HOW TO RESTORE

Sheet Metal Bodywork

OSPREY
RESTORATION
GUIDE 6

HOW TO RESTORE

Sheet Metal Bodywork

Bob Smith

First published in 1984 by Osprey Publishing Limited
27A Floral Street, London WC2E 9DP
Member company of the George Philip Group
First reprint spring 1985
Second reprint spring 1986

Sole distributors for the USA

Osceola, Wisconsin 54020, USA

British Library Cataloguing in Publication Data

Smith, Bob
  How to restore sheet metal bodywork.
  —(Osprey restoration guide)
  1. Automobiles—Bodies—Maintenance and
  repair—Amateur's manuals
  I. Title
  629.2′6′0288   TL255

ISBN 0-85045-591-X

Editor Tim Parker
Associate Graham Robson
Design Gwyn Lewis

Filmset and printed by
BAS Printers Limited, Over Wallop, Stockbridge, Hampshire

Special thanks must go to the staff of RS Panels, Nuneaton and to
Practical Classics magazine

CONTENTS

Introduction

The bodywork of a car is the feature which so often obviously cries out for restoration. It doesn't matter how well-loved a car's chassis and running gear may be, but if the bodywork is scruffy, then the car will always look a mess. A lot of work—hard work and often boring work—is always needed to bring a car back to its 'as-new' condition, but the effort is always worthwhile.

Osprey asked me to prepare this book, about the restoration of the bodywork, because it's my profession, and because after 30 years in the business, I still enjoy the work. But this means that I have to be careful in offering advice to anyone setting out to restore their very first car—for what might look easy enough to me, might look dauntingly difficult to them.

In this business, to tell you what has to be done is straightforward enough, but to tell you exactly how to do it is impossible. Experience counts for almost everything, and nothing beats a great deal of practice. What I mean is that although anyone can talk about shaping and planishing panels, welding and brazing, replacing or repairing sections, there is as much artistry as hard work in the process—and you can't teach artistry through a book. Many people with the right tools can change a clutch, or set up a front suspension, but reshaping a complex panel, or recreating a rusty sub-assembly, just isn't as simple as that.

It took me a long time to become competent in working metal, and restoring or rebuilding bodies, so I ought to mention how I came to specialize in this trade. I've always lived in Nuneaton, which has had engineering links with the motor industry right from the start, and I spent six years as an apprentice in a small company building car panels. One important job was to make parts for Reliant three-wheelers, another to make the aluminium roof panels for Morris Minor Travellers.

I stayed with that firm for three more years, then 20 years ago set up my own business. At first I concentrated on car repairs, but before the end of the 1960s I started restoring and recreating complete bodyshells—and that's when it started to get exciting! Now, if you visited my workshops, you wouldn't only find Ferraris, Jaguar

Which is worth restoring, which not? How many of these old wrecks can be rescued for further use? With skill and experience, you can achieve miracles

E types and more modern cars being restored, but you might also find completely new shells for obsolete cars like Jaguar C types and Aston Martin DB3Ss taking shape.

I haven't written this down just to boast, but to point out that I now know what is needed, in terms of space, facilities and equipment, to do a proper job of restoring bodies of all types. One important lesson I have learned, incidentally, is that bodies are bodies, no matter what the badge on the front, or the price paid for the car. The heartening message I can give to a would-be restorer, therefore, is that it is never more difficult to restore an expensive car than a cheap one (unless the corrosion has gone much further, of course). In fact, you will often find that the construction of the 'hand-built' cars is a lot more simple than that of mass-produced machines.

The first point I must make, and you'll find I repeat this often, is that there are no short cuts to the business of restoring car bodywork. I'll bet that almost every 'abandoned restoration' advertisement in the motoring magazines has been caused by a private owner getting frustrated by the time it is taking him to do the job—and he has found that the first work he ever did is needing rework before the last sections have been done! So, unless you only have to deal with one small section of your car (but I would not be surprised if, under the paintwork, there is more work than the obvious to be tackled), come to terms with this—it will *always* take a lot longer than you hope, you will *always* uncover more corrosion, damage or previous bodging along the way, and you simply won't *believe* the amount of elbow grease and back-breaking toil which is eventually needed!

You will not be able to tackle a major rebuild without a certain amount of preparation, or without buying (or hiring) some equipment, but at least there is no high-technology gear involved. Almost every resourceful home mechanic with a roomy garage, light and power, should be able to do his own work.

A professional restorer's workshops—enough to make any keen amateur go green with envy. The bodyshell is for an Aston Martin DB3S, and a variety of panel work is coming together in the background

I would say, however, that he should not try to straighten out a car whose bodyshell, or body-chassis unit, has been twisted or racked in an accident. It is one thing to set about restoring a body which is basically straight

and sound, but it is very difficult indeed to straighten out the structure first. Unless the shell has been properly straightened out on a jig, don't attempt to do it yourself.

Nor am I going to give advice about the restoration of main monocoque structures, or 'chassis legs' which you find in the underside of unit-construction bodies, for that is to be covered by another book in this series.

The most important item of equipment you must have, is a spacious garage. It would be very difficult to tackle all the welding, reshaping and repair of panels, the bolting and unbolting of things like doors, bonnets and boot lids, unless you have room to move around. You don't really need a pit but what you do need is elbow room. A double garage, with only the one car in it—placed properly—will suffice, just as long as there is space for all swinging panels to be opened wide, and there is sufficient ventilation to get rid of the noxious fumes generated in the work.

I don't need to stress, surely, that the atmosphere should be as reasonably dry as possible, for a damp atmosphere, open to the elements, will play havoc with your efforts to keep a bare shell rust-free before you have time to get the necessary protection on to the surface. Which means, of course, that it makes no sense to start rebuilding a bodyshell in the open air, even if you cover it over with a tarpaulin most of the time.

The workshop or garage you use should have good strong lighting, preferably strip lighting for universal illumination, and modern (13 amp, ring main, in the UK) electric power circuitry, so that you can plug in fires for local heat where needed, and plug in welding machinery and other power tools.

Everyone needs welding equipment, because without that you can't tackle anything. This means that you need gas-welding gear, and preferably some form of spot-welding equipment as well. For pure repairs, and many restorations, gas-welding will do every job, but if you are a stickler for originality then spot-welding will be needed where it should be reproduced. Gas-welding gear can deal with both steel and aluminium work—it's just a matter of setting the flame properly in each case.

The average home mechanic won't be able to get true

professional gas-welding equipment, for he would have to
deal directly with a company like British Oxygen, but
there's a lot of other good gear on the market. Ask around,
and you'll soon discover a local supplier. Also, don't forget
that you can't usually find cheap stuff that is any good—
you get what you pay for, and must pay for quality and
durability.

Gas-welding involves using a mixture of two gases—
oxygen and acetylene. There's no substitute for acetylene
or for the high-pressure bottles it comes in. Although you
don't need a licence to store it at home, I'm sure that the
local Fire Brigade would like to be informed. They would
advise you on storage precautions, and of course they
would strongly recommend that you have powerful fire
extinguishers on hand. Tell them what sort of welding you
will be doing (and, therefore, what sort of flames will be
involved—deliberately or accidently!), they will advise on
the best extinguisher for your purpose.

As far as it goes, the budget-price spot-welding equipment available to most amateur rebuilders is good value,
but it doesn't last long. The professionals' equipment is
very expensive, and unless you intend to tackle a series of
restorations it probably isn't worth buying it all. Better to
use gas-welding instead, and make a really neat job of it.
Home-use spot-welding gear, however, gets its power

Restoring and reshaping body
panels, even for a sports-racing
Ferrari, takes time, skill and
patience, but not a lot of
expensive equipment.
  In the first picture above, this
was the state of the Ferrari 250GT
Breadvan before I started work on
it . . .

. . . in the second the crumpled wings and nose sections had been cut back . . .

from a normal domestic 13 amp ring main, so you won't be faced with expensive extra wiring in the garage.

Now, forming tools, the thing here is to improvize wherever possible. Theoretically you need something to fold straight edges and to tackle the production of single-curvature shapes. You can't accurately form curved shapes without a rolling machine, and while you may not want to buy them, you must at least find access to one—they are just like big mangles. *Don't* try to use anything not strong enough for the job and *don't* go out to buy a new one—you can't afford it! Look for a second-hand one where dealers sell second-hand machines. A quite flimsy rolling machine, perhaps with three foot rollers, may only cost £150, and you'll be able to sell it on afterwards.

There *are* such things as folding machines, of course, but here a bit of resourceful improvization works wonders.

... and in the third the new panelling was beginning to take shape. With aluminium, as with steel, you can weld, beat and form the new areas in smaller sections

For sure, you can make do with an angle iron clamped to a work bench, and that will be quite good enough for most single-restoration jobs.

I don't think there is any way, or any point, in trying to get a big, heavy wheeling machine, which is essential for forming double-curvature shapes. In any case, they don't seem to be made new anymore, and good second-hand ones are in short supply, and expensive. Forming double-curvature shapes is not for the learner, in any case—I'd rather recommend that you buy replacement panels, or pay to have them made, than trying to tackle your own work here.

For small areas, of course, where you have to patch, it is amazing how you can improvize by the traditional Italian method of using hammers, planishing tools, blocks and a block of wood. You'd be amazed just how often the trade still does this.

Buy the best and most versatile power drill that you can find. Not only will be essential for the conventional jobs, but it will also be needed for using sanding or cutting discs, and for chasing rust out of certain areas of the body. There are specially-profiled drill bits, by the way, which we use all the time for getting through old spot-welds without going right through the other panel; they are what we call centre ground drills, and they have a very flat profile.

Although we use power hammers, rather like the Kangos used by builders, for cutting along seam-welded edges, these are powered by compressed air, and need expensive equipment. There are electrically powered equivalents, which you could investigate, but in many cases you can achieve the same result by flame-cutting old panels away, literally by melting the panels away with a really hot gun.

For the hand work, you will need a good range of hammers, files, dollies, tin snips and the like. Rather than my listing exactly what you need, I suggest that you strike up an acquaintance with a local specialist, and not only find out what he uses, but where he gets it from. The metal-working tools *are* available from specialized hardware shops, but you have to find the shops first!

Equipment for solid rivetting or pop rivetting will always be valuable, but most well-equipped amateur workshops will already have that sort of thing on hand, and you will need a good selection of metal-working drill bits.

I'm sure, too, that you will already have invested in good protective clothing for all the restoration jobs on a car. For restoring the bodywork, there's really no need for special heavy-duty clothing, but you should have good overalls, boots or shoes which will give your feet some protection when you drop sparks (or metal panels!) on them, and good gloves and goggles for the welding process.

Finally, one good way to learn the basics of the craft, before you start making mistakes on your own car, is either to help a willing (and tolerant) friend with a similar task, or to enrol at a local technical college for an evening class on welding or on metal-working. As I have already said, there is no substitute for experience and practice. If you don't want to do this, or don't have a course close enough to your home, at least you should start work on scrap panels or scrap pieces of metal; that way, you can get the feel for the hand tools and discover if there are others that you need.

Apart from the welding equipment and, I suppose, the right size of garage for the job, you don't need a lot of up front capital to tackle a bodywork restoration, but up front expertise is invaluable.

I'll tackle the sourcing of new materials—steel and aluminium—in the chapter on repair or replacement, but now it is time to get down to the hard work of panel preparation. If you don't have a backache already, you certainly will have by the end of the next chapter!

Bob Smith

Chapter 1 | Strip down

Oh dear! This is the sort of mess which may be exposed when the body strip down gets well under way. Basically, though, this Triumph TR4A floorpan should be restorable, once you have cleaned off all the rust and the paint, especially as the car relies on a separate chassis frame for its strength

If you are proposing to start the restoration by stripping down the car in your own workshop, you have missed out several important steps! First of all, at the very beginning, you should have gone over the car with scrupulous care, even before you signed the cheque, and drove or trailered it home. Unless you knew you were proposing to buy a 'basket case', you should have poked and prodded all around, not only with the proverbial screwdriver (which is absolutely infuriating to the man selling you his pride and joy) looking for rust and thin patches, but with a small magnet, which would help you locate unexpected and unwanted patches of filler or fibreglass.

Let's assume however, that you have bought the car, or that it is a car you have owned for some time. The first questions you should ask yourself are: 'Is it complete? Is it all there?' It is most important that you have a complete car, for in some cases finding new or replacement panels can be very time-consuming, or sometimes plain impossible. Incidentally, I don't just mean that the bodyshell should be complete, but that all the decorative items—trim strips, badges and other exterior items—should be in place, or at least supplied with the rest of the machine.

In the case of some cars, you have to make a big decision even before buying one at all. Should you get a reasonably good car which might have parts missing, or made non-original, or should you settle for a scruffy car which you can see is absolutely complete but in a bad state? It depends on the known state of the parts-supply market, of course, but in the case of older or rarer cars, or those where the 'classic' potential still has to be recognized, you should never count on finding the bits you need. It is far better to accept a real dog of a machine, as long as every component is present.

(An acquaintance of mine recently bought an otherwise good Jaguar SS100 sports car, found that he needed a new tail lamp assembly to finish off the job, and was appalled by the rarity, and the price asked, of the replacement item.)

It follows therefore that I'd always counsel extreme caution when buying a 'basket case' of a very rare car, for when you get it home you might find a few baskets missing!

When you are ready to start work, look before you touch, touch before you start to strip out, and assess the overall prospects and problems before you get too involved. Now is the time for another determined poke around with the screwdriver, inside and out. What you see when you are buying the car, and you may be a bit over-excited, is not what you will find when you have had a proper chance to look around.

Study it well, get a good idea of the basic build-up, whether the wings are bolted on or welded on, whether the engine will have to come out upwards or downwards,

Such partly dismantled bodyshells (this is a Jaguar XK120 coupé) look discouraging, but at least in this case almost all the panels are available to the restorer, and are basically sound

Above **If a panel has to be scrapped, there is no point in taking ages to get it away from the bodyshell. This BMW coupé front wing is being chiselled away, and will not be reused . . .**

Right **. . . having pulled it away, a lot more trouble was exposed underneath, so perhaps it was the best course of action after all**

Above right **Minor repairs are being carried out to this Austin-Healey 3000 with the rear wing still in place. But if the wing itself is detachable, and needs work, that too should be detached**

whether you can remove the doors from their hinges, then plan how you are going to begin to strip down. Make notes—all the time—and make sketches as well. It's all very well stating confidently that you will always remember how some parts fitted together—you won't!

If a complete body restoration is going to be needed then strip out the shell completely; if one section only needs to be done, completely strip out that area. It *is* worth it, believe me, and there are no short cuts. If you leave trim, or electrical wiring, or hydraulic plumbing in place, it could be damaged by heat or flame in the welding or repair processes which will follow.

Before doing any strip down, it is well worth having the whole car steam cleaned, for this will remove any grime, caked mud, and other debris that has become stuck to the shell over the years. It will also expose some obvious corrosion patches that you might otherwise not have stumbled upon until much later in the process. It is easy enough to find steam cleaning agencies, for most garages dealing with trucks have this facility, as do those dealing with heavily-waxed cars brought in from overseas. Costs are very reasonable, and in the long run it tends to save you a great deal of time.

Start by removing all the trim, interior and exterior, and this includes all the badging and bumpers (especially plastic bumpers), then follow up by removing the lamps, glass and brightwork. As you do so, use a series of big cardboard boxes (food shopping at supermarkets is an ideal source) for storage. Mark up one box, say 'Left front door', and put everything from the door in that box. Label up small bits with tags so that they will not be lost, take lots of pictures if you can, and add notes and sketches. You have no idea how confusing it will look in 12 months' time when you come to start reassembly! Small sub-assemblies can still get lost in the jumble, so I recommend bagging them in plastic bags; freezer shops are an ideal source, or padded envelopes are a good alternative.

If you are working on a tight budget, it might make sense only to work on one section of a car—front end, doors, tail or whatever— at any one time, but normally I wouldn't recommend it. You may find, that way, that the restoration

Right **A full strip down usually reveals all manner of horrors under the skin. This is the outer face of a Jaguar XK120 footwell/ bulkhead assembly, and a lot of work will soon be needed to make it good for the future**

Below **Stripping out a Ferrari 275GTB door, glossy on the outside, showed that the inside was in a bad state. It also showed that this particular Italian supercar had very crude drop window fixings, and other details. At least we were easily able to get at most of the bits and pieces**

The same Ferrari 275GTB, this time the boot corner, seen from the wheel arch. Even on these cars, anti-corrosion protection is not all that good, and after less than 20 years the metal had rusted badly, with holes right through at the corners. The wheel arch edges, too, will need patching, and filling, before a reassembly can start

Even before all the paintwork and gunge was removed, it was quite clear that the entire boot floor on this car was about to fall out, for there were long cracks at the corners. A completely new floor was eventually needed

Above **Rust is heavily advanced
around the panel joints of this
Rover P4 saloon. You will
probably not discover the true
extent of the problem until the
paint and all the protective
underseal (if any survives) has
been removed. In this case,
though, the lower panel is welded,
not bolted, into place**

Right **Look before you touch, then
strip before you repair. The rust
around the side/indicator lamp
apertures can be removed,
stopped and the panel repaired,
but you will have to take away the
lamp unit before starting work**

of your pride and joy is never complete, for the first part tackled may need doing again by the time you have finished the last, as your standards might have improved a lot, or the corrosion might have set in again. . . . In the end, I reckon it would cost you more.

Many cars seem to have major bolt-on, rather than weld-on panels, which makes stripping out that much more easy. Cars like the Rover P6 and Citroën DS19 saloons had every skin panel removable by finding the appropriate bolts, but a majority of cars have bolt-on front wings, and most moving panels can easily be removed too. In many cases, it makes sense to mark up the exact position of hinges before you loosen off, or setting-up door gaps and other clearances will be a lengthy business at the reassembly stage.

If a car is less than 20 years old, most bolts can usually be loosened. Odd ones will always break off, in which case

Below right It is tempting to try for a 'temporary repair' with a GRP filler, or even extensive lead-loading, but I wouldn't recommend it. It is better, by far, to get the glass and its rubber surrounds out of the way, before seeing how far the damage has progressed

Below Mud thrown up inside the wheel arch of a car like this Rover P4 may have clogged behind various lamp housings, and provided an ideal breeding ground for corrosion. First of all you must strip out all the components, then you must start removing all muck, debris and paint

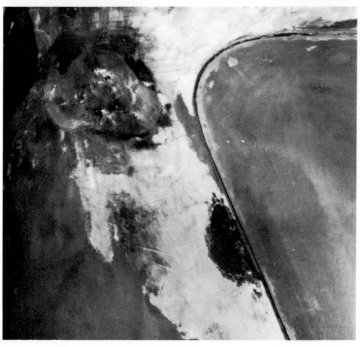

Left **As with the Ferrari, so with this Jaguar—the boot floor is just about ready to fall out, and if it habitually has to support heavy loads it will surely do so! It's probably not even worth attempting a repair here, if a proper replacement panel is available instead**

Below left **Lots of filler, and maybe lead-loading as well, around this bonnet hatch, will all have to come off straight away, before you can assess what has to be done for a proper restoration**

Above right **A real mish-mash, isn't it? The outer sill and the door sill is new, but there's a lot of corrosion on the door pillar, and rear wing. At least, in this state, you have just about got down to rock (or rot) bottom**

Below right **All the paintwork, trim sections and door furniture has been removed, to expose this horribly rusty door pillar. Unless the pillar is dangerously thin after all these years you should be able to patch successfully, but since this is a stress-carrying area, don't be tempted to 'make do' with lead-loading or a GRP filler**

Below, far right **The inner wheel arch looks ripe for complete renewal, though the door might be repairable after a lot of diligent stripping, and careful reworking**

you'll have to drill them out and remove the broken part; there is, however, an extractor tool, rather like the reverse of a tap, with which you drill, then 'tap' the broken end— you screw it in *anti*-clockwise, and eventually the tool removes it.

Rust-remover, liberally applied, often helps, as does heat from a welding torch, and you can always be patient and use penetrating oil.

Incidentally, even if you cannot find a way of getting a door off its hinges, or hinges off the bodyshell, you can usually get the hinge pin out, for it is usually split, made of spring steel, and can be drifted in or out.

Even at this stage, you should be assessing which panels or sections can be repaired, or which will have to be renewed; it may not be immediately obvious in some cases, but my advice is that as soon as you know what new parts or panels will be needed, you should order them straight away. This will save endless hours of waiting when the time comes to start reassembly. In general, though, you should wait until the paintwork and other protective materials have been removed, and you can get a good look at the state of the steel or the aluminium.

If you can get a quick impression of what is not worth preserving, the strip down need not be a very skilled operation. If a panel is quite obviously scrap, have no mercy on it—cut it clear, perhaps with the heat of a welding torch, and get on with something else which takes more time. Be decisive, but be sure! The main tools are the welding torch, the spot-weld remover I have already mentioned, spanners and screwdrivers, a hammer and chisel, and some hard work.

Store big panels—bonnets, boot lids, doors, and removable wings—well out of the way of any walkways or doors, so that they don't sustain any unnecessary damage by being kicked or scraped around. A loft above the workshop is an ideal place, but not the pit (if you have one) for that means the panels might then be peppered with other items being dropped from above. If there are fixings to go with a particular panel (such as hinges, fixing nuts, and special attachments), bag them, and fix the bag securely to the panel by tank tape. If one bag is remote from its panel,

This Ferrari 250GTO bodyshell has been completely stripped down for investigation. For a car of this quality, and rarity, such a drastic operation was amply justified to see what has been exposed

by definition, it is misplaced. In the typical workshop, mis-placement is half way to having something lost for good.

At this point, your precious car will look as if it has been attacked by an efficient team of vandals. Fear not. Things can get worse—and they are about to do just that. Having stripped out the shell, we now have to get down to bare metal to assess the corrosion problem!

Chapter 2 | Cleaning off

Before dealing with the corrosion to steel or aluminium panels, you must tackle the messy job of cleaning off all the paintwork, anti-corrosion material, and everything else getting between you and the clean bare metal which has to be exposed, before you can begin to rebuild.

I never recommend partial removal of paintwork, for it is usually difficult to achieve a perfect match of colours only by respraying part of a body. In my business, we would always want to take all the paint off the bodyshell.

The way to remove paint, quite literally, is to use a good paint remover, it's as simple as that. I don't mean to be at all condescending, or pedantic—it *is* the easiest method, and quickest too. To strip a complete car may take more than ten litres/two gallons of the stuff, so don't buy in penny numbers. You have to brush on the stripper—it's a lot like wallpaper paste in consistency—and a two inch brush will do nicely. Incidentally, we start by pouring from a 5-litre can into a smaller tin, then use the brush from that; the brush should never be used for any other purpose. Probably the best way is to tackle one area at a time—a door, a front wing or whatever—so that you do a good job, and don't miss anything.

The strippers to use are dual purpose, and can deal with most types of paint. Sometimes it takes time to react, but at other times the paint starts to bubble up and loosen off almost at once. Generally though, if a car has been painted two or three times, you have to soak the stuff in, leave it for hours, then go right round again before the paint starts to lift.

Really you should wear protective clothing—rubber gloves and glasses, certainly, and preferably an overall—

Above **Even with new panels, or sub-assemblies, it may be necessary, sometimes, to clean right down to bare metal to make final repairs or adjustments. This Jaguar E type bonnet needed accurate fitting to the scuttle panels, and work was also needed on the doors. Not a pretty sight at this stage, perhaps, but to an experienced restorer it is all beginning to look good**

Left **On this Jaguar XK120 FHC, the strip down of the offside front wing shows up several types of old repair, and a patch panel under the vent, towards the door opening face . . .**

for although there is no major health hazard, splashes can be very painful. If the stuff gets on your skin it stings, and it can be dangerous if it gets in your eyes. Don't delay after an accident—wash in copious amounts of water immediately, and don't skimp on the rinsing out.

In most cases, the paint remover will produce sheets of paint peeling off the car, so you should ideally have started with newspaper, or preferably grease-proof paper, all around the car on the floor of the workshop. Go round each panel with a scraper, lifting off the paint, and deposit it on the paper.

The exception is modern acrylic paint, which the right sort of paint remover turns into an absolutely unspeakable gunge that just runs down the panels and drips on to the floor or paper.

By the way, one very good reason for stripping out a car before you apply paint remover is that the remover can be absolute death to some components. If you splash it on perspex sidescreens, back windows or other such trans-

. . . which with a lot of detail attention can be made into a sound base for glossy new paintwork

parent panels, it reacts very quickly and very badly with the plastic, and it cannot ever be cleaned off.

In all cases, get rid of the remains by burning them, paper and all, in the open air. You'll get some smoke, and the smell isn't nice, but that is the end of the trouble. Never pour the stripped acrylic mess down a drain, and don't just toss out the removed sheets of paint for the dustman. Don't do the burning in an enclosed space, for obvious reasons.

It's very important to get every last bit of old paint off a body panel, very important to get it absolutely clean. After getting the paint off by conventional means, you might then find body filler, or some sort of undersealing, exposed. One of the easiest ways of lifting this stuff is to apply a blowlamp to heat it up, then use a scraper to move it—but be careful, as filler is very flammable. In any case, you'll get a lot of smoke and strong smells.

Generally, though, I wouldn't recommend using a naked flame to soften up paint before stripping it off, as it would be very messy, and the heat might tend to distort the panel shape, especially if it is thin steel or aluminium.

To get at the tar-based underbody sealers though, use

Sand-blasting, by machinery brought to your own home, is one service offered to restorers. Treat this with great care, however, particularly if your car's body panels are in aluminium, for it can do quite a bit of damage, especially if the panels are thin and fragile. Personally, I would not recommend the process

Right **Aubrey Finburgh looking over a rather tired Jaguar C type rear end, preparatory to starting the manufacture of new replacements. At this stage there is a mixture of paint, filler and some corrosion dotted around the assembly! The AC Cobra nose, behind the Jaguar panel, is new and just about ready to be offered up to the chassis**

Above, far right **Are these surface bubbles in the paintwork, or does something more serious lurk underneath? Nothing less than a complete clean off, first of the paintwork, then of the underlying corrosion, will tell the whole story**

Below, far right **There is a lot of filler in evidence here—signs, perhaps, of an earlier 'bodge' repair. For a permanent restoration, you will have to get rid of all the old filler, and see if the remaining panel is worth repairing properly**

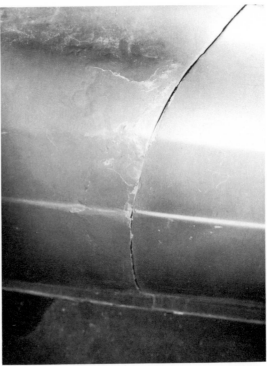

Above **Two adjacent Jowett Javelin steel panels, with flanges turned in, will need all the paint removing, inside and out, before you can see how badly the flanges are corroded. With luck this car can be repaired and patched— one hopes so, for new panels are no longer available**

Above right **A good puzzle here for detectives—door/wing gaps all wrong, cracks in the wing surface and much filler in evidence. It should all be stripped out, and the paint and filler removed, before the necessary remedies can be decided**

the blowlamp approach, with a scraper. Warm over a section, not so that it begins to burn but so that it becomes soft, and then it should come away from the panels with the aid of a scraper. Really this is a two-handed job, not because you can't do it alone, but because there should be company on hand to move things along more quickly, and for immediate help if a small and localized fire does break out!

You will notice that I haven't yet mentioned sand-blasting as a means to getting paint of a panel. That's because I think you could end up doing more harm than good to the metal panels themselves, particularly if they are aluminium (which, compared with steel, is relatively soft). The only case for sand-blasting, in my view, is if good strong panels are involved, if they are not exterior panels, and if you cannot get at some paint, or other covering, by any other method. But remember this—that blasting can destroy panels just as easily as it can strip them. . . .

Unless you have a car that has been meticulously and honestly maintained, you are almost bound to come across areas of fibreglass used to patch (or, if I was honest, 'bodge') repair. You can lift fibreglass off with the aid of the blowlamp, but it is highly flammable, so you *must* have a friend standing by with a fire extinguisher, just in case. If you can, perhaps, get the metal warm by heating it up from behind, then the patch might loosen off without danger, and a scraper will do the rest.

You are also likely to find quite a lot of lead-loading used on older cars, sometimes to cover up earlier corrosion which was 'restored' some time ago. The trouble is that although the lead, once in place, will not corrode (it is inert in that respect), the steel underneath can keep on crumbling away, and once you remove the lead there might be nothing but a lattice of nasty thin steel underneath. To get the lead off, use a blowlamp until it liquefies and runs away—it isn't flammable.

But there is a potential health hazard with lead, so if you start discing and filing the stuff, with particles flying through the air, I recommend that you wear a face mask.

Most suppliers of paint, the under-paint preparations,

The rear wing of this Aston Martin DB4 is not in bad condition, as a searching removal of the paintwork has revealed—just a few local problem spots which will need attention right away

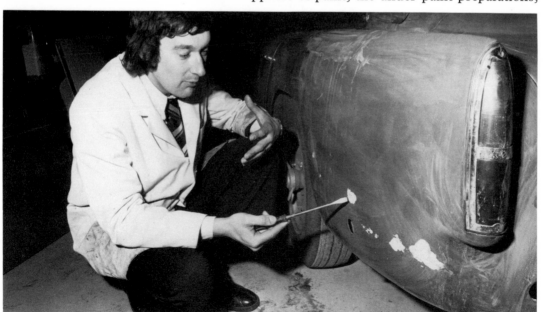

The finger points at body-to-chassis mounting points on the floor pan of this Triumph TR, which are in bad condition. You must certainly not attempt to bodge here. A lot of work, too, will be needed to the panel above these mounts

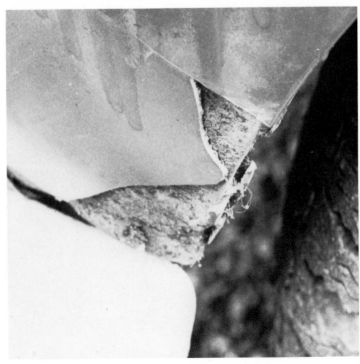

There is a lot of thick old filler here, with panel rust obvious below it, where it has chipped away. What a horrible sight—a previous 'temporary' repair has lived up to its name. It will have to come off

Right **The dreaded tin-worm has had many fruitful years to attack the metal surrounding this headlamp, and I suspect that by the time you have chipped away at all the rust, there will not be a repairable panel left over!**

Below **An innocuous looking rust pimple, when scraped away, may turn out to be much more serious—as this one was, and the problem hasn't been 'bottomed' yet. Keep going, until you have exposed sound metal**

and rust-protection compounds, also sell all the brushes, clothing and masks which you are always going to need, so at the start of your first restoration, find a good supplier, and stick to him.

I would never recommend the use of a power-driven disc to remove paint, not only because it takes a long time, and you get through a lot of discs, which get clogged up, but because it can damage the panels themselves, particularly if they are thin due to rust—before you know what happens, you might have sliced a hole in a panel, and ruined it. A power-driven sander is quite useful for removing filler, which is a chalk-type material, with fibreglass in it, but it creates a lot of dust which gets everywhere, so once again you ought to wear a face mask to protect your lungs.

Inside the bodyshell, often on the floor panels, or the inside of doors and the boot compartment, you might find pads of material used for sound-deadening and damping. Normally these will be hard and brittle (having become so over the years), and the way to get them off is by using the blowlamp and scraper approach again, or a bolster-type chisel.

Only rarely will you find panels actually glued together (one example on Aston Martins of the 1960s was that inner and outer skins of bonnets and boot lids used to be glued together), for most use a metal-to-metal adhesive allied to clinching of one panel flange over the other, or conventional welding. In any case, paint stripper will not penetrate to that glue, and you should never have a problem.

By the time all the paint is removed (and the last patches will have to come off with hard detailed work, perhaps more local use of paint removing compounds, scrapers or even rough paper—but always be wary of causing surface damage to the panels themselves), you will have found other material which has to be removed. If you find steel panels which literally have to be chopped away from others, and are not spot-welded, you may have to take a decision to scrap them, or to cut away the patches of weld with aid of a power-driven grinding disc. Don't use a chisel, especially a power-driven chisel, unless you have no alternative, for it can cause a great deal of damage and really is a Stone Age method.

Finally, to clean off the body after you have used all the paint strippers and abrasives, you can use water if the stripper was water-based in the first place; though obviously it must be dried up immediately, otherwise you have provided the ideal conditions for rust to start up before your very eyes. Instant heat helps, of course.

In my business, we tend to use petroleum-based thinners and wire wool, and it's a long and tedious business. You need to wear rubber gloves, have the thinners in a tin (to be painted on with yet another brush that you don't use for anything else), and the wire wool to work over the body, removing loose paint and any little bits still sticking to the bodywork. Then wipe off each panel, after you have done this, with a clean rag.

So far, so good, but you now have the bodyshell at its most vulnerable state. Now is not the time to delay, or to go on holiday. The forces of evil—rust and salt corrosion—are *already* at work against you. Tackle the corrosion problem right away!

Chapter 3 | Rust and aluminium corrosion—the treatment

This is where the back-breaking work really starts. You might already have spent a great deal of time stripping out the bodyshell, and getting rid of all the old paint and other coatings, but now you have to get the panelling really clean. As you read on, you will realize that there is just no substitute for lengthy toil, for you simply cannot rely on a chemical miracle to sort out the rust, and the aluminium corrosion.

Which reminds me that I should make it clear that aluminium does deteriorate, if not as severely as steel. If your car has aluminium panels, they stand a better chance of being in good condition after years of rugged use, but you will still need to work on them to get them back to as-new condition. With steel the obvious—*very* obvious—problem is rust, while with aluminium it is corrosion encouraged by road salt, or by electrolytic action at panel joints with steel. I will deal separately with the problems, but in many cases the abrasive treatment has to be the same. That aluminium doesn't suffer is a myth, for the formation of aluminium oxide, a white looking powder, is quite irreversible, and eventually it weakens the metal.

First of all, though, let's talk about rust and how to get rid of it. Every steel-bodied car, from Mini to Rolls-Royce, suffers to a greater or lesser degree, and only the very latest cars (such as Porsche 911s) with galvanized panels, seem to be immune. For our purposes, we have to deal with two basic types of rust—one is the heavy scaling and pitting brought about by years of exposure to wet roads and clogging mud, the other is the light dusting of surface rust which seems to take hold of a panel even when it is only a few days or weeks old.

In the last chapter, I suggested that you should make decisions about scrapping badly mangled panels even before you start work on them, and I now give you the same advice regarding panels which have been badly rusted away. Unless you know that replacement panels cannot be found, it is rarely worth your time and effort to slave away at a panel which, when cleaned up, might be dangerously thin in places (or even have holes needing patching). It will be far quicker, cheaper and safer just to fit a new panel instead, and I would only modify such advice for a fanatic who wants to keep his car as 'original' as possible.

To get rid of heavy scale, the only sensible method is to use wire brushes, on an electric drill if you can get in to the affected area, or by hand if you are unlucky. There is no magic chemical to do the job for you, though some have their uses for light rust, as I will mention later. For the heavy stuff, you have to treat it with muscle power, either your own or that of the electricity board.

It's all hard work, with no science at all, and none of us enjoy it. That's why the poor apprentice usually gets the job, when he is beginning to learn the trade!

However, you have to be careful where the rust has gone a long way in to a panel and the sound steel may have become thin. A rotary disc can be powerful and it is all

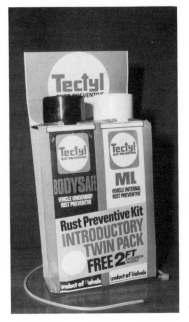

Above **The best time to use rust protection compounds is after all the existing rust has been removed, thus not trapping any old corrosion under the surface of the preparation. Tectyl and Waxoyl are just two of the many available treatments**

Right **One good, reliable but arduous way of removing corrosion, is by using a wire brush**

Right **Rust is not too badly established here, but all the paint and all the existing corrosion will have to be removed before new panel protection and paintwork can be applied**

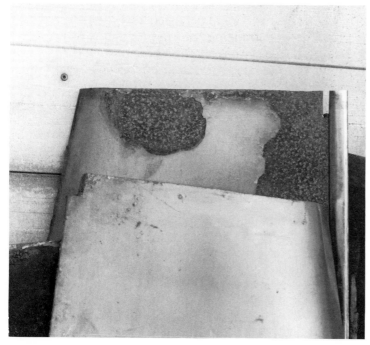

A comparison of different panels, the badly corroded type never having received rust protection and prevention treatment, the other (the same type, from the same car) having been treated, and having fared much better

too easy to rip a hole away. The consolation, though, is that such a panel is usually too far gone to be worth restoring and ought to be renewed. In delicate little corners you will either have to do the job by hand, or very carefully with a small tool, but in all cases you *must* 'bottom' the rust in a dry process, or it is all going to be a waste of time in the long run. The best way of encouraging new rust to start, after a rebuild, is to leave some existing rust in place. In this business, near enough is not good enough—it must *all* be removed, and this just needs lots of hard work, and friction, I'm afraid.

There isn't much point in trying to get rid of awkwardly placed rust by burning it off (although this does work, up to a point), as the heat tends to distort the shape of the panels while you are getting rid of the rust. It might be the idle man's acceptable method of heavy-gauge chassis members, but not at all on body skin panels. I don't recommend it.

Even so, it will be difficult to remove every speck of rust, and at this point you should turn to the use of chemicals. A warning, however—don't expect this stuff to get rid of heavy scale, or really solid deposits. The chemical reaction is usually by neutralizing the rust (which is iron oxide), but the inert iron compound formed tends to form a barrier between the outside world and any deeper rust which might not have been neutralized. With heavier deposits, therefore, the rust-remover might actually be harbouring deeper rust, which can then carry on proliferating at its leisure. One way to minimize this possibility is to brush on the rust-remover (which is a liquid, as supplied in a can), then when it has done its job, brush off the resulting compound and repeat the whole process.

In my particular business, we are now using a commercially available preparation which was originally developed for use on oil rigs and ships, where the salt-laden atmosphere really was death to steel. It is actually a primer as well as a rust-remover, and is guaranteed for 15 years. It isn't cheap, but the claims for its life span are impressive. By the time that this book is published, such preparations may generally be available. By the way, as with most such things, you get what you pay for—the best, and the most carefully developed, usually cost more than the catch-penny rubbish.

What happens after the body is completely clean really belongs to a book on paintwork, already published in this series, but at this point I ought to comment on rust-proofing preparations which have been so controversial in recent years.

There is no doubt in my mind that such preparations, *if properly applied*, can be invaluable. The problem is that many such treatments are sold out, by franchising methods, to inexperienced operators, some of whom are not as honest as they should be, and their efforts are sketchy, to say the least. That explains why more than one concern has been forced out of business by excessive warranty claims, and why the trade has got something of a 'cowboy' reputation.

The fact is though, there will be some parts of the body where rust will have taken hold, and which you can't get at—I'm thinking particularly about the inside of box sections, body sills and complex little areas too close to the splash areas, which could harbour mud and general road

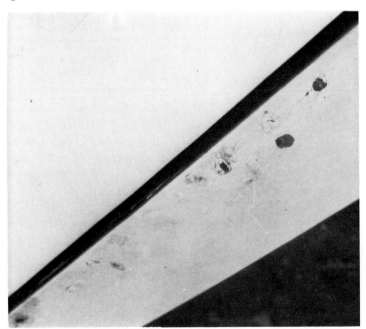

This looks like surface rust only, which you should be able to confirm when all the paintwork has been removed. By building up the surface coatings from clean base metal, you should be able to guard even against this in the future

Bodyshield professional operator about to drill into a body box section, to apply anti-corrosion compound

filth. The only answer is to have such parts treated with a reputable treatment, like Waxoyl, and hope for the best in the years to come! Incidentally, the car you buy might already have been treated—you can usually detect this by the small plastic plugs in hinge or door faces, or by seeing brown streaks around panel joints, for they are applied from a spray gun at high pressure.

(The 'cowboys', by the way, thought nothing of drilling and adding the plastic plugs, but not actually bothering to spray much rust-proofing compound inside the section. . . .)

To make sure that rusting does not happen again, clearly it would be nice to think about galvanizing the steel (Lotus do this with chassis frames, and Porsche and Volvo are also great believers), but it is impracticable for complete shells as they used to be dipped in baths of liquid. On the other hand, it *is* practical for removable panels like wings, or for new panels you have not yet welded into place, but it isn't cheap and when you weld it the protection is destroyed.

Similarly, there really isn't much justification in trying to use stainless steel panels instead of mild steel—for one reason, pressings of this stuff are just not provided, and for another stainless steel is more difficult to work, and more brittle in any case.

There is one process which my own business is now using for some parts, that of aluminium spraying (the aluminium is fed through a gun, melts in the heat and is sprayed on in particles), but it makes a smooth finish almost impossible on an exterior panel. Really this should only be considered for parts of the underside, where it can't be seen; it isn't feasible for larger panels.

One of the most difficult areas to locate and get rid of rust, is in between panel joints, for instance where one panel is spot-welded to another. You have no choice but to remove rust around the joints, and when you are rust-proofing at a later stage, hope that some high-pressure fluid can be forced into place to do its job. But it's a thankless task—consider, for instance, the external seams on Minis, as just one example.

Now, let's talk about aluminium. Quite a lot of classic cars have light alloy skin panels—bonnets, boot lids and doors, mainly—but just a few have even more extensive

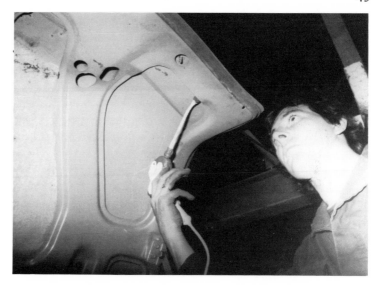

To corrosion proof properly, it is necessary to get the fluid, under high pressure, into every nook and cranny, such as the inside of this double-skinned panel

aluminium skinning. Land Rover enthusiasts, of course, will know that the bodies of their machines are almost entirely built from aluminium alloy as well, which explains why it is very difficult to wear them out!

Generally speaking, aluminium panels are a lot thicker than steel ones, but as the metal is so very much lighter, there is still a considerable weight saving in the end. By this time in the restoration, you will already have discovered—if you did not already know—that most aluminium sheet is also quite soft, and quite easily dented or otherwise damaged; incidentally, Land Rover panels are much more robust than any other type.

Aluminium, compared with steel, is more reluctant to rust, but once the crumbly white aluminium oxide powder has begun to appear, it seems to get through the panel rather more quickly. Once you discover that aluminium corrosion is present, it is highly likely that energetic strip down and cleaning will reveal holes! Compared with steel, by the way, it is much more difficult to patch alumimium panels, but I will deal with that problem in the next chapter.

To get rid of aluminium oxide corrosion, proceed in general as you would do when getting heavy rust off steel, but take more care because of the softness and relative fragility of the aluminium, especially in the case of super-sports cars where the panelling is quite thin. The oxide does not stick, or flake, in the same way as rust, so it comes away rather easier. This means that you do not need to use strong-arm tactics, or he-man powered rotary discs—be gentle to start with, using fine sand paper, and you will be happy to see the oxide lift off quite easily.

Once you have got rid of the corrosion by this method, or with hand scraping or sanding, that is the end of the process, because as far as I know there is no chemical equivalent to a rust-remover to get right down into the pores of the metal. By the very nature of the corrosion, and the aluminium itself, you will effectively have done that with the sanding.

Aluminium corrosion starts where salt spray has got at unprotected sections—paint damage due to flying stones is an obvious point—but it also tends to begin at the edges of panels, where they come into contact with steel panels. A type of electrolytic reaction occurs, and a low electric current is set up across the joint (that's nothing to do with a car's normal earth-return circuits, of course), and the aluminium begins to oxidize, to form the familiar white powder. The steel doesn't suffer at that point, though.

One way to make sure that electrolytic action does not occur again, after you have cleaned up the mess, is to interpose a barrier-type of cloth adhesive between the joints, a process used by Aston Martin, among others. Most aluminium panels are bolted, or rivetted, to a steel structure, so in the course of a rebuild you will almost certainly want to remove them. When the time comes to start reassembly, stick this tape to the appropriate steel surfaces, before you offer up the aluminium panel for its permanent location. Unfortunately, this tape doesn't last for ever—it tends to go rotten, like most things on a car—but it really does help stop the electrolytic action.

There are other proprietary barrier paints on the market, though these are not easy to find, and I don't think they are as effective. Incidentally, one reason why barrier paints or barrier tapes eventually become ineffective is that they may become worn through by the relative movement between the metal surfaces. On some older cars, with separate chassis, it is quite amazing just how much 'working' and flexing of bodywork there actually can be.

As with steel, so with aluminium, it is worth having the panels properly protected once they are thoroughly clean, and down to fresh metal. Clearly the galvanizing process will not work for aluminium, but any of the reputable rust-proofing sprays are worth adding to the aluminium, just to set up a barrier. With aluminium, you see, it's not water you need to keep away from the metal, but salt. If you are lucky enough to live, and drive, in a region where there is no seaside spray, and where the local authority does not salt its roads to melt the ice during the winter, you are luckier than the rest of us.

All the signs, by the way, are that the painstaking business of corrosion removal will not need to be done as often in the future as it still is today, for more and more car manufacturers are adopting really stringent body protection processes when building the cars from new. Six year corrosion warranties are now common—if not written down, then effectively in force—but to get your money back in case of trouble you must still have subjected your car to regular annual inspections.

So much for the preparation, which has taken a good deal of time. Now it is time to start the reconstruction process.

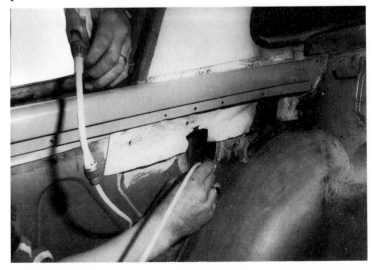

The area between inner and outer wings is highly vulnerable to rust on all cars. but it can usually be treated once trim panels have been removed

Chapter 4 | Repair or replace?

As I have already advised, you should really have started to order new panels even while the strip down was in progress. But I can quite understand if you were too involved in getting rid of all the old paint and protective gunge. Now, however, with the bodyshell laid bare and all the corrosion chased away, you have to start making decisions, in every part of the car—are you going to repair and patch up, or are you going to fit new panels?

This depends on several things, and obviously the time factor involved is far more important to a professional, or a body-making concern, than it is for a private owner. In other words, we always have to ask ourselves if it is cost-effective to patch—will the labour costs involved make it worthwhile?

But a vital consideration, particularly for older and rarer cars is—are new panels even available? For a Jaguar E type, an MGB, or any other classic car made in big numbers and now supported by established specialists, a large variety of new panels are available. But for almost any coachbuilt car, or a limited production machine like a Ferrari, or a special-bodied Alfa Romeo, Lancia or Fiat, it is highly unlikely that you would ever find spare panels.

In almost every case, therefore, I would recommend that you buy new panels, instead of trying to patch up badly corroded old ones—unless you want to be able to boast about the car's originality when the restoration is complete. Even a private enthusiast, after all, ought to weigh up the fact that to spend up to 50 hours repairing a panel may not make sense compared with spending £50 on a new panel, and perhaps less than a day fitting it.

Where we would have to spend ages fabricating a com-

Above **Once you have decided to fit new panels instead of badly corroded examples, be ruthless in removing the old ones. In this case, the operator is cutting off a front wing, using a power-tool**

Left **In many cases, these days, remanufactured panels have been made available for cars which have been out of production for many years. The entire rear end of this Jaguar XK150 shell was pressed and welded up in the 1980s**

Right **This is an increasingly rare example of a shell built up on the basis of a wooden body skeleton. It is sometimes difficult to remove existing panels to repair them without damaging the wood, but welding repairs close to the wood would otherwise be potentially hazardous**

Below **Before starting to make up panels for your old car, or spending many hours repairing the old panels, try to find out if replacement panels are still available. In many cases, items such as these (actually for Jaguar XK120s) are available 'off the shelf'**

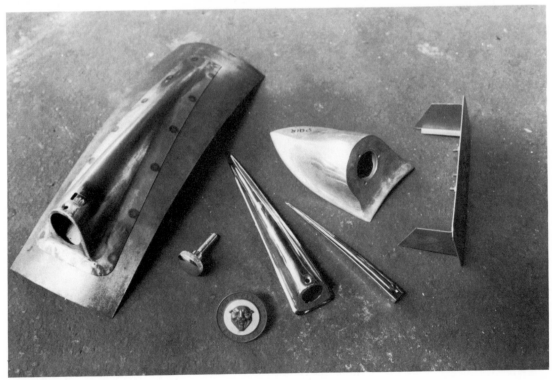

Many reputable remanufactured panels, or part panels, are available for popular cars, such as this MGB GT. In the case of the MGB, note that the rear 'wing' is actually a part-panel only

plex new double-curvature panel, my establishment tends to patch the corroded sections instead, but even that involves quite a lot of careful shaping of a patch, welding into place, smoothing out the joints and generally finishing off.

First of all, however, assess the state of your car's bodyshell, and in particular be ruthlessly practical about the strength of the panels which have survived extensive rust removal. Even though a panel may be absolutely clean after all your work, it might have become thin and rather weak. Therefore, decide if you want to keep a panel which is somewhat flimsy and which in all probability will eventually rust through, years before the new panels you decide to fit to other parts of the car.

Next, make sure that you know where all the best sources of replacement panels are located—and by that I *don't* mean where the cheapest panels are to be found. The one-make clubs usually have a fund of knowledge about their own cars, but I'm afraid to say that they often tend to recommend the cheapest and not the best.

We live in a competitive world today, so it is not likely that many specialist panel suppliers are making a killing

We were rather proud of this at RS Panels, for most of this Jaguar D type shell and monocoque was newly shaped and assembled on our premises. Note how we have built up large areas of panelling—like the front wings and the bonnet sections—from small sections, but welded together

at their work. Accordingly, you tend to get what you pay for—a cheap panel could just be cheap *and* nasty, whereas a more costly one has probably been shaped on properly developed tools (or even on original presses, bought from a manufacturer when he abandoned the support of the car in question). The panel is only as good as the tool used, and if time has not gone into its refinement, the panels will be below standard.

There is still a great deal of rubbish about, I have to say, not because of the material quality, but because of the shape and the detailing. Superficially they might look right, but on several occasions I have found it impossible to fit them to existing bodies and had to discard them in favour of a new panel from a different source. Sometimes I have suspected the body of being twisted, but it always proved to be the fault of the replacement panel itself!

How do you pick the good from the bad? Really, this cannot be done visually, so if possible you should learn from other peoples' experiences. If you can, get to know a restoration specialist who has done a lot of jobs, or another enthusiast for your model of car who might already have tackled his own rebuild. In the end, this could save you a great deal of time, money and frustration.

Although I will sketch out the ways in which you can start shaping new panel sections in the next chapter, all in all I would say that it is never worth your while to do this unless you are sure that you cannot find ready-made panels or sections instead. If you don't have time, but you have the money (lucky man!), tricky aspects of this work can always be contracted out to the specialists—but expertise does not come cheaply.

There is a possible alternative, if 'your' car is quite rare. That is to buy a derelict body (or 'basket case' car) which is not worth restoring in itself, but which has sound, or basically sound, panels which you need. I know it's a pity, and that the stock of historic cars is going down all the time, but this method at least allows one excellent machine to be recreated out of two or more very poor ones.

You cannot rely on a manufacturer keeping stocks of panels for many years after a car has gone out of produc-

This Porsche 356 was hit up the back by another car, and needed a lot of repair work on the tail. Remanufactured panels did not seem to be available and it was not practical to repair the crumpled remains, so we had to make up new shapes and weld them to the existing shell

tion. Soft trim, I agree, is the first to disappear from factory lists, and engine parts seem to go on for ever, but well within ten years you might find that pressings go 'out of stock', and are then abandoned. In recent years, specialists have tended to buy up the last run of panels from a manufacturer, but they can rarely afford to take over the press tools to make more when that stock has been sold out. This means that the most determined specialists then have to start remanufacturing panels, which usually means that they have to make a big investment in temporary tooling, for a limited run.

In most cases, replacement panels tend to arrive in only a partly finished state, which means that you may have to consider drilling, or slotting, for certain decorative strips and patches. Manufacturers do this not because they are idle, but because one basic pressing (a door skin, wing or boot lid, for example) might have different decoration for a different model derivative. On European Ford Capris, for instance, some doors had brightwork strips along their

The sills of this Austin-Healey 3000 were beyond redemption and are about to be cut away to make way for new panels. It was thought to be quicker (and therefore more cost effective) to take this action

creases, and others had stuck on decals, while some had door mirrors and some did not.

Panels which need clinching over, or which may need detailed work on their flanges, are sometimes supplied without the flanges already turned over. You will have to tackle this yourself.

Even if you decide to buy new panels, rather than make your own, at a very early stage you should decide how many new pressings you need, and find out what alternatives are available. It is often a false economy to buy a small repair section, but on the other hand it is often worth buying a section rather than a complete panel.

Obvious examples here are that manufacturers provide either complete wings, bottom sections of wings or perhaps extreme (front and rear) sections, to suit where obvious corrosion points become known. You can buy new sections, say, for the front corner of an MGB wing, which tends to go rotten around the direction indicator lamp aperture, or just one half of one side of the floor-pan of

It is certainly worth repairing, rather than replacing, the inner and outer wings of this Triumph TR3A, though it will be necessary to strip back the paintwork to good, fresh metal to make sure of this

Above **No more than minor repairs, perhaps not even any patching, will be needed to make good here. Before even starting to buff off the paintwork, feel carefully around the inside of the panel for further evidence of decay**

Right **Having removed the front wings of this Austin-Healey 3000, corrosion to the inner wings/ shroud can also be noted. In this case, however, it should be possible to make fairly simple repairs on the flat flanges**

Above **This outer sill is in the traditional 'muck and bullets' area, and is much more corroded than the floor pan inboard of it. It can't be repaired, so a new panel will be needed.**

Left **This is scandalous. The outer wing was welded in place only one year before the picture was taken, the flanges completely unprotected against rust by a 'cheap-and-cheerful' repair. Nevertheless, repairs should be possible—but I hope it will be better done this time!**

Above **This is all that was left of
the front corner of a Fiat 2300S
Coupé after 12 years. No easy
repair was possible—new patch
panels had to be devised**

Right **The boot floor of this
Triumph TR was holed and
wafer-thin everywhere. It didn't
make sense to patch repair, a
complete new panel was
required. It was no more
expensive and quicker to fit as
well**

a Jaguar E type. You can buy almost any 'corner' of the back panel of a BL Mini, where the normal panel is large, and completely surrounds the boot lid. You can even buy some panels or sections as small sub-assemblies, where a side (parking) lamp housing might already be welded into place.

I know that motorists criticize the insurance companies a lot, but they must take the credit for minimizing the amount of new panelling which has to be bought for a relatively minor crash repair.

In the case of complicated sub-assemblies, like bonnets and boot lids, you usually need to purchase them already welded up (inner and outer), but more and more these days one is able to buy door skins only, to weld into an otherwise sound door structure. As far as I know, outer skins for bonnets and boot lids are never supplied.

Many cars have their door glasses surrounded by light metal extrusions, not pressings, and if these are damaged, they are the very devil to repair. These are never available as separate items either, so if new extrusions are needed, it usually means that a complete new door, or the complete reconstruction of the door, will be needed.

On most bodies, some of the panels rely on special fixings to attach them to the car—cage nuts, hinges, strikers or spacing panels. These are always sold as separate items, and are often difficult to find if the car is old. Generally speaking, though, they are not as flimsy (and therefore not as likely to rust away) as the main panels themselves, so you might be able to repair them.

In many cases you will have to repair them, or you may even have to think about improvizing from more readily available parts from other cars. If the result is going to be hidden away, and you don't tell the Concours judge, I think that is perfectly acceptable! In many cases, by the way, things like cage nuts are common to a complete manufacturer's range of cars, which might give you another clue for hunting, and in the case of bodies which came from one independent body builder (such as Standard-Triumph, Rootes and BMC products from Pressed Steel Co. in the 1950s, or a whole variety of General Motors products from the Fisher Body subsidi-

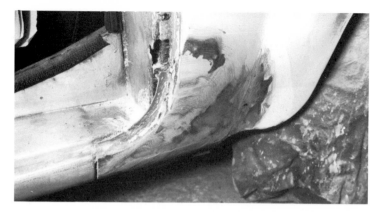

ary), the choice and the possibilities might be even more varied.

Now for a few words about patching, though I will go into more detail on welding in a later chapter. First of all, decide (as I have outlined above) that you really do need, or want, to patch. Then, even though the panel is completely clear of rust, cut the panel further back, either to a convenient joint, or section change, to completely sound metal. Remember that corrosion-free-steel, if thinner than standard, may not be strong enough any more.

By definition, a patch panel, or the new section you have made up yourself, will be larger than the gap it has to fill—a bought panel is almost always going to be considerably bigger, even if it is a popular type of repair section. To fit one to the other you should always lay the patch on to the remainder of the panel that you intend to retain, trim it neatly back as far as you want, then scribe a mark on the existing panel and cut that back to suit.

Above right **The lower rear wing of an MGA, close to the door aperture. The outer wing is basically sound, but quite a lot of patching will be needed to the door shut face**

Left **The nasty state of a sport's car's inner panels when the outer wings had been removed. Complete new sills had to be fitted, and extensive repair work was also needed to the inner wings**

Never do this with the original panel (if, say, it is a wing, or a sill) removed from the car, as the original might not then be taking up its proper shape, and you could have all kinds of fitting problems when you do come to offer it up to the car. My advice is always to use the existing body, and the existing chassis frame, if the car has a separate one, as its own jig.

Once you have trimmed one patch or repair panel to suit the rest, you should butt-weld the one to the other (I will cover this in a later chapter). It might look easier to joggle one section to go under or over the other section, to gain strength, but this is not necessary, it adds complication and it is actually no stronger than a simple butt-weld. This advice applies especially to aluminium, where a joggle really needs to be rivetted together, and for an exterior shape that is just not sensible. In no case do I think you need any extra strengthening panel behind the butt-weld; if the butt-weld is competently done and properly finished off, you should never have any more trouble.

I have already made it clear that I do not recommend a beginner to try to shape large areas of panelling himself, especially if there is any question of double-curvature involved. Incidentally, if you have a chance to look at a large new panel, or area of a bodyshell, which has been built up by experienced specialists, you will find that it

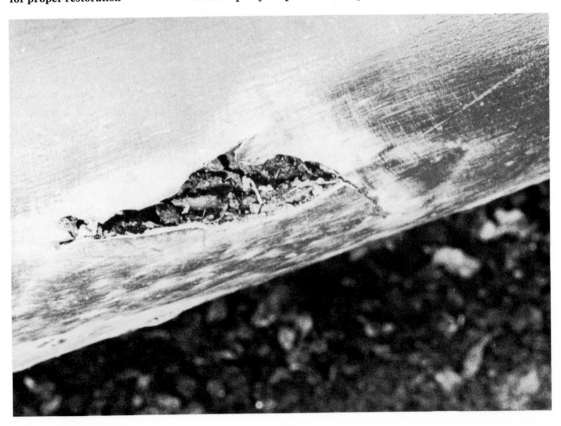

Looks like a rat's nest, doesn't it? There is lots of old filler here which will have to be removed. Probably an entirely new panel— a sill, in this case—will be needed for proper restoration

often consists of several smaller sections, neatly butt-welded together. Something long and sweeping like the nose of a sports racing car might have at least half a dozen separate pieces.

Finally, before I leave this section, a few words about the merits of steel and aluminium. Of course, if you worry about originality, you should never even consider replacing one material with the other (unless, as with MG bonnets for example, you know that both types were used from time to time). You cannot weld one material to the other, so you should only consider fitting aluminium wings—say—instead of steel, if they bolt on to the main shell. I don't recommend using aluminium for any panels which are structural (which means that they impart bending or torsional strength). If one panel is spot-welded to another, it invariably means that it has a stress-bearing structural job to do, and since you can't spot-weld steel to aluminium, that should convince you quickly.

However, it is a fact that aluminium is easier to work, and it saves a great deal of weight. For some panels, therefore, *if* they can easily be fixed, rivetted or bolted to the rest of the shell, *if* they are not likely to be damaged or distorted by regular use, or by accidental clouts, and *if* originality is not a problem, then consider aluminium as an alternative to steel. (In any case, it is much to be preferred to fibreglass replacement. . . .)

Unless you have bought accurately profiled panels to fit into your car, you will now have to tackle the job of working the metal, preparing it for assembly or even to tackle the shaping of new patches. That, the material you need, and the tools required, are what the next chapter is all about.

On this door thick filler has been used as a bodge, but the panel has almost completely rusted away underneath—a completely new skin, at least, will be needed to make good

Chapter 5 | Shaping new panels

I have not been looking forward to writing this section, as it covers skills and operations that cannot really be taught through the printed word. When it comes to shaping new panels—either for patching, or complete panels—there is really no substitute for experience. I can summarize by saying that you will not be very adept at first, and that you will continue to improve with practice. I learned my basic trade over six years as an apprentice, but I am sure I am still adding to my experience today.

However, if you are determined to make some of your own sheet metal, I think we should start by discussing, briefly, the materials themselves—sheet steel, and sheet aluminium. First of all, where to go for supplies?

It isn't as easy as it sounds at first, for you simply cannot waltz down to your local car parts supermarket and pick up keenly-priced sheets of the metal. The easy way—the short-cut way—is to get to know other people who have already done the searching, or even find a local commercial specialist, and ask them where their supplies came from. Main steel stockists are few and far between, and you rarely find companies advertising. However, look in the telephone book *Yellow Pages*, either under 'Steel stockholders', or 'Sheet metal work', and you will usually find a contact address close to your home.

At companies like this, sheet metal is often available in standard sizes—say 2 m × 1 m, or perhaps 8 ft × 4 ft. You might decide to buy complete sheets, or you might ask for a smaller piece to be cut off for you, if that is all you need. The costs are not too frightening, for flat sheet. Clearly these vary from country to country, especially as inflation keeps dragging down the value of money, but steel cost

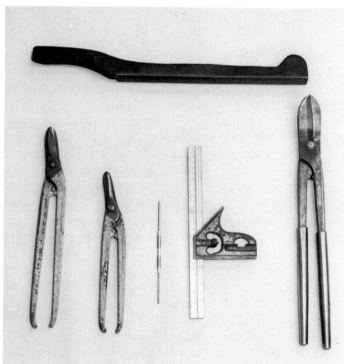

Above **This selection of panel beating tools should cover most tasks. In the centre is a selection of different shaped dollies, flanked by the various types of hammer. Note that the hammers should be used only for panel beating, and should have a smooth, mark-free face**

Left **Most cutting and trimming jobs, not forgetting marking out, can be done with these tools, but I'm sure you will build up more as your experience grows**

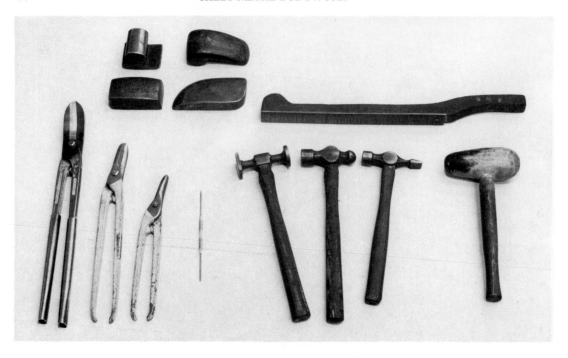

well under £1 per square foot in 1983 (most thicknesses),
and aluminium was perhaps 50 per cent more costly than
that. The value of a panel is not in its basic cost, but in
the time and expertise which goes into shaping it!

The normal material specifications for the sheet metal
used for exterior body panels are CR4 steel (that means
'Cold Rolled, Type 4), or SC1 aluminium, both of which
are normal commercial type materials, with no special sort
of anti-corrosion protection. Some British postwar cars
used what was called Birmabright aluminium panels, but
there was nothing special about this, as it was merely a
trade name, probably because the Birmingham Aluminium Co. supplied the stuff.

Even in this day and age, sheet metal is still sold in
various thicknesses identified as 16SWG, 20SWG or
whatever, where SWG means 'Standard Wire Gauge';
usually the stockists themselves just talk about
'20 gauge'—so you will have to learn to pick up their
jargon! Incidentally, the smaller the gauge 'number', the
thicker the panel, which sounds Irish. . . .

If you have access to a wheeling machine, you'll find it very useful indeed for coaxing sheet metal into the desired double-curvature shapes. But it all takes time, and a lot of experience and patience

Generally speaking, steel body skin and non-structural panels are 20SWG or 22SWG (which is 0·036 in. or 0·031 in. thickness, generally called '36 thou' or '31 thou'), while most aluminium panels are in 16SWG, which is 0·064 in. Although it would save you money, and weight, to buy thinner gauge material for the rebuild, you would automatically be opting for panels more flimsy than before (and more prone to rusting or corroding through, in due course), so I don't recommend that you do this.

The stress-carrying sections of unit construction car bodies such as the 'chassis legs', major cross members or the big stiffening box sections on the underside, are invariably made from much thicker steel, 12SWG or 14SWG on older cars, but probably 16SWG or 18SWG for more modern, more scientifically designed, bodies.

Recently, cars like the big Volvos, and the latest Porsches have been specified with galvanized steel body panels, but you will very rarely encounter such materials in cars

Wheeling machines, if you can get the use of one, are very versatile. Different sets of rollers allow different curvature radii to be persuaded into a sheet of metal

that need total restoration. Frankly, I do not think it worth buying galvanized sheet when restoring your car, especially as the treatment has to be destroyed during welding operations, and the fumes produced are toxic.

There is however, a special steel much used these days, especially where a car has suffered serious structural repairs and failed its fitness tests, called 'Zintex'—but once again, local welding burns off the zinc coating, and leaves that part of the panel just as vulnerable to rusting as normal mild steel.

Aluminium sheet does not suffer much when stored for a period before you shape it into car panelling, but steel certainly can. To store sheet steel, try to find a dry place (outside, or even outside under a tarpaulin, is *not* good enough!), and smear it all lightly with a film of oil, as a barrier against moisture. The good news is that this helps a lot, but the bad news is that it all has to be cleaned off again before use; always work steel in the dry state.

Even before buying new sheet, however, you should have made the basic decision about the value of restoring compared to using new panels.

In this chapter, we not only have to consider making new panel shapes, but we have to consider reshaping damaged panels, and even patching what is left. (I discussed the way of preparing a panel for patching, or for the use of repair sections, in a previous chapter.) I know that many enthusiasts want to keep as much of the original bodyshell as possible, but I really think you should always ask yourselves the oft repeated basic question—is it worth repairing or should you just get a new panel?

You must always use your judgement, which comes from years of experience, to see whether you can cope with a repair. Badly crumpled or torn panels could take you 50 hours of toil and aggravation, and you still do not get a panel looking as good as a professionally pressed new

Left **No matter how you choose to shape or reshape metal panels, it is always advisable to check the progress of the work as you do it. In progress here is a fairly simple front wing panel, for which a wooden former has been made, and for which the workman has also cut out a simple template**

Below **The operator is shaping a new panel on a wheeling machine, but to his left is a former which was made up to reproduce the exact shape required. In that case, a simple steel 'honeycomb' has been made, but you could also get away with a plywood 'box' if no more than one or two panels were to be made**

panel. Of course this applies more obviously to a skin panel than it does to something less accessible like an inner wheel arch, or inner boot panel, or a boot floor. But think about it—always. Then think again. Your time may not be money, as it is in my business, but you should always consider the *total* time you are likely to spend on a restoration.

Next, let's consider tools, and equipment. I'd better make it clear, right away, that you should not begin to consider working metal with nothing but ordinary hammers. Metalworking need not be a very capital-intensive business, but there are certain items that you will need to do a proper job.

You can economize, however, on marking out equipment. There are adverts for instruments 'specially developed for metalworking', which is true as far as it goes, but you can easily get away with your old school geometry kit, if it is robust enough. Naturally, the more tools you have, the easier any job becomes, but if you have good steel measuring tape, or rulers, and a simple scriber, that will help enormously. Incidentally, you will see some people saying that a nail, or a screwdriver is good enough without buying a scriber, but is it really worth penny-pinching to that extent? (If you must pennypinch, take a tip from some of my panel beaters—they sometimes used sharpened up broken hacksaw blades!)

You will need files of various finishes, of course—but you probably already have these in the workshop—a pair of good, strong tinsnips for cutting off excess metal, or for roughly trimming a panel to size before you begin the detail work, and hacksaws for making a more accurate cut. A power tool with a variety of cutting, grinding or smoothing discs will also prove to be invaluable.

No doubt you would be green with envy if you walked around my workshops, but there is absolutely no point in my recommending that you buy some of the kit we use. For one thing, there is no such thing as a cheap DIY wheeling machine, and for another the type of rolling machines we use are far too big and costly for a private owner to buy.

But a small rolling machine and a small metal folding device may be worth the expense, and you should also

All the elements of 'classic' panel beating are in evidence here—the wooden former for the desired shape, the hand-crafting of the sheet metal, and the ubiquitous tree trunk!

investigate the purchase of a 'joggler'. They are available in many countries—only recently I saw adverts for a 'panel flanger' in a USA enthusiasts' magazine, for $29·95, and they are certainly available in the UK, although you will have to read the trade press.

It is essential, however, for anyone intending to tackle metalworking and restoration to have a good kit of hand tools. One British magazine which often carries news of such items is *Practical Classics*, which offered a really useful set of tools as a special incentive not long ago. There were three different hammers and four dollies, which would certainly have covered most eventualities, and cost only £17·95—the normal retail price of them all would have been more than £36.

Wait a minute. The meaning of 'hammer' is obvious enough, but I know that some people don't understand what is meant by a 'dolly'. The word 'dolly' has grown,

The simplest possible former to use when panel beating is a tree trunk. At this stage, obviously, the shaping is preliminary and a lot more detail work will eventually be needed

over many years, to mean a carefully shaped piece of metal used to support a sheet of metal while you are working it with a hammer.

Basically the way to reshape metal is to hit it with a hammer. (That statement is much easier made than actually doing the job, but we'll come to that later!) Occasionally you will reshape a panel by tapping away with a hammer 'on the wind', which is the trade name for having nothing behind the panel while you work.

In almost every case, however, you set about reshaping a panel as a two-handed job, by having the metal dolly behind the panel, supporting it closely and by hitting the panel from the front with a hammer. Dollies are held in the palm of the hand, and come in various shapes and sizes, the different shapes being so that they can fit under most contours. Ideally, a dolly should be almost the same shape, or a similar shape, to the panel profile you are trying to produce—in effect you are using a hammer and the dolly, two-handed, as a sort of press tool in miniature.

Hammers come in various shapes too, some with round, nearly flat heads, others with square heads for working into sharp corners, some with—literally—pick-shaped ends for really confined spaces, and some with more domed heads. In every case you should suit the hammer you use for a particular local application, and you should *never* use a panel beating hammer for any other job.

A hammer and a dolly should have the smoothest possible 'mirror' finish, and if they ever are damaged, you should smooth them down at once by grinding away the imperfection. Any damage on the face of the hammer will be reproduced on the panel itself, every time you hit it—the problem being even more marked (literally!) if you are working aluminium, which is a lot softer than steel.

The heads of panel beating hammers tend to loosen off after a time, as ordinary hammers do. Keep a close check on your tools and rectify the looseness. The tendency of the heads to wobble about on the shafts could mean that you end up marking the panels every time you strike them.

Three different types of panel beating hammer which you will find are called 'bumping', 'body' and 'pick'. The bumping hammer is the heaviest duty type, used first if you want to get a body dent somewhere back to the right shape before detail work begins (you might use a big 'Universal dolly' instead . . .), while the body hammer (often with a round head at one side, a square head at the other) is used for more detail planishing. Planishing, by the way, is the professional word for the whole process of smoothing out the body profile and producing the shapes you need, using a hammer and a dolly together. The pick hammer usually has a round head for conventional planishing, and a small pick-shaped head for working away in sharp or tight corners.

None of these panel beating hammers is anything like as heavy as one we might use for hammering nails into wood, or whatever, because in general you are never going to need the same amount of force. In fact, I would never recommend that you try to 'make do' wih ordinary hammers, which are not suited to the purpose of reshaping skin panels. For reworking heavier-gauge structural panels, which are outside the scope of his book, such a hammer may be useful.

By the way, useful equipment to help you bend, or shape, sheet metal doesn't have to be factory made. I always used to improvize like mad when I was learning, and my panel beaters do so to this day. They tend to accumulate things—bits of bent iron, straight bits and useful radiused lumps, all of which come in useful.

Many things are useful to help you form single-curvature radii—a large oxygen bottle, for instance, a beer barrel, a hefty fencing pole or even a tree trunk. Trees, in fact, are very useful indeed, for you can even make useful depressions in them, into which you can beat an approximate panel shape. This is the way a lot of the old craftsmen, in the old coachbuilding days, used to tackle their repairs!

Now let's talk about the basic possibilities of reshaping a panel, or repairing the dings and dents which an old car may have suffered over the years. As I have said, if a panel is badly creased or torn, you should consider getting a new panel, but with a great deal of practice you should be able to tackle dented wings or doors.

The first thing you should always do is to look, carefully

and at length, to see how the dent actually occurred. Sometimes, of course, you will know what happened for you damaged the car yourself, but in other cases it is sometimes possible to see the way in which the wing was damaged, and from which direction. You then start planning how to push the metal back, literally, the way that it was distorted. You need to do a bit of detective work, and if possible you should try to reverse the process.

Unless it has been a fierce impact, the steel (or the aluminium, for they both tend to react in a similar way) will not have stretched, so it ought to be possible for an experienced operator to work, or beat, the metal back into its original shape. However, even if there has been some stretching, on a bulbous panel (like a Morris Minor front wing, as a good example) it should be possible to 'lose' it in the end, for a little extra fullness will usually go unnoticed.

To reduce a bump or bulge, always start from the underside if the dent has gone inwards, or the outside if it has been pulled outwards, and try to bump out the majority of the damage, either with a dolly or a hammer, striking in the opposite direction to the way the damage seems to have occurred. After a time, you will find that one good blow in the right place will restored much of the shape, all at once!

After that, experience and patience comes into play, and as I wrote at the very beginning of this chapter, I really cannot tell you in one or two paragraphs how to do this. I often say that the best way to get started, to get your expertise, is to make friends with your local scrap-yard merchant, get his permission to practice on some quite worthless bodyshell, kick or bang a dent into a panel, then practice straightening it out again! It's all going to take time, but eventually you will come to agree that it is worthwhile.

Once the majority of the damage has been restored to a near-normal shape, it is time for the long and patient work to begin. I'm no masochist, by the way, so I always try to get myself comfortable before I start out on this. If you are working on a wing, make sure that wing is at a comfortable height for you to sit on a stool or a bench;

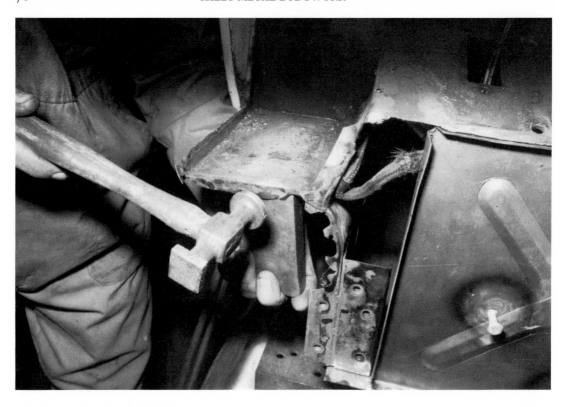

The two-handed use of a hammer and dolly, to 'dress' a flange when restoring a body panel. In fact this job is being carried out on the shell of a Jaguar E type

if it is too low, then arrange for the whole car to be jacked up on good secure stands (no piles of bricks, please!), and if—say—an axle, or the front suspension gets in the way, then dismantle it all.

For all but the last detail touches, by the way, I recommend working on a panel while it is in place on the car, for the rest of the bodyshell will then act as its own location jig. Consider the problem of trying to restore the shape of a complete front wing while it is rolling around on a work bench, for instance. Another important consideration, too, is that you will work best if the panel is held securely, and your arms are not being contorted, or asked to operate at unusual angles.

Even before you start working the remaining damage out of the shape of panel, be sure that the underside is entirely clean. If it is not, every blow with a panel beating tool will tend to dislodge more and more debris, mud or rust scale,

After panel beating, the restored panel should be offered up to the rest of the shell, to see that it fits properly. It is certain that you will not get it absolutely right first time—so patience, and try again!

and if you start hammering away with such impurities still *in situ* you are likely to transfer those imperfections through to the shape of the 'restored' panel.

Having got the worst of the damage out, you will then be faced with a series of high points, and low points—a low point being one where, when viewed from the outside, the metal is still below the required shape of the panel, a high point standing proud. Using the dolly behind the panel (i.e. on the outside, as you will eventually see it from the roadside), start tapping gently, but smartly, with the chosen hammer (probably the versatile 'body' hammer), planishing the material, to get it more and more accurate.

It is all going to take a long time, especially if you are rather timid at first, though the reshaping process is a bit easier with aluminium, which is softer, less rigid and rather easier to work. Eventually, though, you will arrive at a situation where the panel is beginning to look something like

right again, and you will soon have to start checking your
work for accuracy, and surface finish.

Firstly, if the panel was quite 'full'—which is to say that
there was a great deal of shape in it, when properly
profiled—you will need to know if you have returned the
damaged panel to the correct profile. The way to do this
on a car where you are working on a panel at one side, is
to take templates off the *other* side of the car in the right
place (assuming that that side is still undamaged!) in stiff
card, and then match the new shape to the card; vertical
and horizontal templates should be taken, so that you can
be sure. On a boot lid, or bonnet, where there is only one
panel to work on, you may have to find another car like
yours, and take cardboard templates off that.

The secret in panel beating is not to expect miracles to
become obvious all at once, to take time to do the job and
to be as thorough as possible. The best way to wield the
beating hammer is to hold it quite lightly between thumb
and fingers, using that point as a pivot, using repeated relatively light blows rather than hefty whacks, and always to
ensure that the full face of the hammer head makes contact
rather than an edge of that face.

When you have the panel beating job finished, or think
you have finished, go over the area involved with a Dreadnought file and this will soon indicate the remaining low
spots, for the file will not have touched them. Once again
you should concentrate detail work on those low spots,
filler-up again, check that the job is done and call it quits.

There comes a time with any panel beating job where
you are chasing really small improvements, and where you
should then consider getting rid of tiny imperfections with
filler. Don't be ashamed of making such a decision, for it
is one the professionals make all the time. I'm not advocat-
ing filling great inch-wide dents with gobs of filler, or trying to patch up holes with fibreglass, but I am saying that
a smooth, thin layer of filler, carefully applied, will be far
more cost effective in terms of time and expense, then
repeated and finicky panel beating.

It's almost impossible to put a time limit on the work
you can justify in straightening out a panel, though in business we have to make such estimates all the time. After

a lot of practice, you will be able to assess a bump and know whether you want to straighten it yourself or not. If you can't straighten up a wing, say in a day, then I think you should be considering a new replacement panel in any case.

The sort of damage you will always find difficult to restore to shape is that caused by diagonal raking motions, say a bumper carving into a door and leaving a sharp crease or fold. Almost always the panel will have been stretched, and after you have straightened it all out there may be metal left over. Even we, as professionals, cannot easily get rid of that. There is a way, only for experts, where you get that section of the panel red hot, and gradually planish away—literally 'flow' the metal away—until you have the right shape again. But it is often more practical to get everything as straight as possible, with a narrow groove left over, then fill up and smooth over with body filler.

The sight that makes it all worthwhile—this was an Aston Martin DB3S which was almost entirely rebodied in my workshops in aluminium

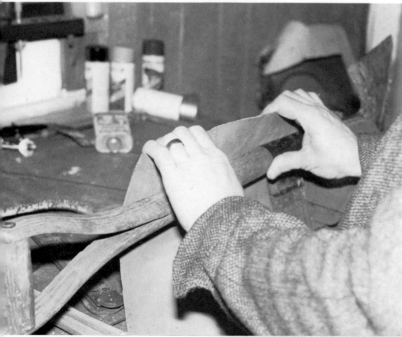

Far left **Simple folding tools like this C. G. Automation bender can help enormously with the shaping of new metal if you have to make straight creases. The panel is inserted, to a carefully marked position . . .**

Above left **. . . and the folding operation does the rest**

Left **When forming metal shapes, be versatile—this particular panel is being bent around the wooden handle of a garden spade!**

There is one instance where it might be feasible to use heat—full red heat in the metal, by the way—and that is if the accident has caused some creasing, which you cannot reduce by cold working, beating and planishing.

It is certainly feasible to straighten out a panel, and then find that one section is too badly mangled to repair—cut it out, and replace it with a self-made patch or by a repair section (already mentioned in previous chapters). However, I don't think you should ever even consider welding a new panel on top of a damaged one. That really is cheating, though I have to admit that I have seen it done in professional body shops where speedy 'MoT' or 'fitness repair' jobs have to be done.

In this case we are usually talking about body sills, but in the end you wouldn't have solved the problem, for the damaged and rusting original panel is still there, under the surface, rusting away and setting up problems for the future. I call that sort of thing bodging, and I'm not about to recommend bodge-ups.

Before I go on to talk briefly about shaping panels from flat sheet, I ought to mention that quite a number of the replacement panels you may buy for a restoration will be incomplete, and will require some panel beating before they can finally be fixed to the car itself. I do not mean that they will have been done incorrectly, but that some flanges may have to be turned, or clinched (if we are talking about door skins), or that some wing edges for older-type cars may have wired wheel arch edges, the last few inches of which may have loose wire protruding, and the arch turnover not completely formed. In every case this has been arranged so that assembly to the car, and the fitting, can be done in the most painless manner.

Incidentally, many of the more individually built cars—Morgans and Aston Martins, to say nothing of ACs, Ferraris and other machines—are *truly* individual, which is to say that a door from one car might not necessarily fit another bodyshell. Specialist suppliers of panels for such cars always allow a bit of extra material, so that it can be tailored to your own bodyshell. Getting rid of extra material is one thing, of course, but finding material to fit an extra large aperture is another thing entirely!

Now, to the shaping of new panels, or patches, from flat sheet which you have bought from stockists. This is not as easy as it sounds, especially if any form of double-curvature is involved. Single-curvature, by the way, means a panel only bent in one plane—a form you would produce by shaping metal around an oxygen bottle is the obvious example—whereas double-curvature is the shape of metal you would have to develop for the front end of a shaped wing pressing (like an MGA, Triumph TR3A or Sprite/Midget).

Any one of you, I would say, should be capable of producing single-curvature shapes, but producing double-curvature requires a great deal more experience, and practice. To form double-curvature panels, of course, our workshops use wheeling machines, and these are simply not available to the average home mechanic.

In either case, I ought to say that there is no shame in deciding to make up a big panel in several sections, even if the original which you are replacing was a one-piece pressing. The original was probably stamped out with the aid of massive press tools, which are quite beyond your means, or those of a restoration workshop. If you were to visit our workshops, and see a Jaguar D type or Ferrari Testa Rossa body coming back to life, you would see that we have built up the shell from smaller panels, carefully butt-welded together. After filing, and careful finishing, no one could detect the joints from the outside view.

If you only decide to tackle the shaping of single-curvature sections, or patch pieces, then it is only a matter of careful and patient forming, perhaps using a portable rolling machine if you could justify buying one, or perhaps by careful panel beating around a suitably rounded object. As I said before, you will need to know what the correct radius or curvature, or more likely what the rather more complex curve, actually is, and the best way to test your panel as it takes shape is to compare it against heavy card, or wood templates, taken from the other side of the car.

For larger panels, or for more complex panels, perhaps there is really no substitute for making a proper jig, but you should then ask yourself if you should not be buying replacement panels instead. But if they do not exist any more—there must be dozens of truly coachbuilt cars (I can think of many postwar Bentleys and Rolls-Royces, for instance), where the original jigs have long since been destroyed, and where replacement panels have never been marketed—you must either choose between putting the job out to specialists, or tackling it yourself.

For the average man, though, I would think that anything much larger than a foot-square panel would be too big, and if it has styled creases, or swages in it, the problem becomes a lot more difficult to solve. His only way would be to make some crude type of former, for him to get the shape approximately right—panel beating could be carried out, from the inside of a panel, into the depression in a tree trunk which he has made (I mentioned this earlier), or perhaps into, or round, a 'sandbag', which is a leather bag filled with sand. He should never try to produce a shape which has a sharp crease, or discontinuity, in its profiles, but should try to produce a panel going up to the edge of that crease, with just enough spare metal to turn up to form a flange ready for welding. The classic case of this on a British car would be the front wing of a Morris Minor with those headlamp pods.

Naturally there are some differences between working steel and working aluminium, generally confined to the fact that aluminium is softer than steel. This means that it is easier to change the shape of aluminium, but it also means that aluminium does not hold itself so easily. You cannot substitute aluminium for steel panelling where the one panel has to be welded to the other, for the two materials cannot be welded together. Aluminium panels can, of course, be rivetted to steel inner panels, but this is always obvious on an inspection, and may not be desirable where originality counts, and in any case the overall rigidity of that part of the car will also be reduced.

Next, however, we are in a position to start welding one panel to another, and this is the subject of the next chapter.

Chapter 6 | Spot-welding

Bodyshells are built up from a number of different panels, sometimes in aluminium (or even, these days, in plastic of some kind) but most often in pressed steel. In the majority of all cases, the steel panels are welded together. Whether a car is built in large numbers, or just on a very small scale, there are two principal methods—those of spot-welding, or electric-welding.

If you are tackling the complete renovation of a car's bodyshell, I am sure that you will want to preserve, or reproduce the original features. This means that you should consider spot-welding panels together if that is how they were fixed when new, and it means that you need to learn the basic skills, and methods, of the spot-welding process.

The problem for the enthusiastic restorer, working from home, is not in learning how to use spot-welding equipment, but what sort of equipment to use. Portable spot-welding equipment which plugs into a normal domestic electric power supply is limited in its scope. The sort of spot-welding equipment used in big repair garages, or in specialist businesses like my own, tends to be heavy, expensive or needs industrial capacity wiring.

My advice would be to hire, rather than to buy, a spot-welding machine, for I don't think most people could justify spending a lot of money on equipment if they are only intending to tackle one major rebuild. In fact, if you only have a limited amount of spot-welding to be done, it might even be worth your while having it done, rather than tackling it yourself.

You cannot, for instance, buy a good spot-welder for much less than £225, unless you manage to pick up a

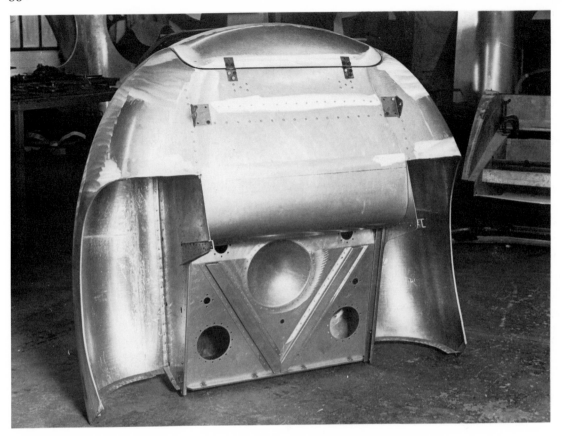

Spot-welding, professionally done, 'stitches' neat lines of weld to fix panels together. This is the rear end sub-assembly of a Jaguar shell, almost ready for finishing operations to begin and paintwork to follow, and is a clever mixture of welding and riveting

second-hand bargain, perhaps in a liquidation sale, or from a business which is re-equipping with more modern, technologically-advanced equipment.

One of the important problems with spot-welding equipment is in gaining acccessibility to the section to be welded. But, on the assumption that you can get the tips of the equipment to the flanges in question, I would always recommend spot-welding rather than electric-welding. Not only is the result as strong as anything you can achieve by other methods, but it is usually far neater as well.

Portable spot-welding equipment usually has a range of different shaped tips, in a variety of shapes, so that you should be able to get to most places on the body which need welding. Obviously, if it would mean straddling a big expanse of floor pan to get to a panel joint on the trans-

mission tunnel, even the biggest and most expensive mach-ines couldn't cope.

The obvious easy places for spot-welding are simple panel edge joints and flanges (for example, the exposed flanges on Minis, or where inner sills meet outer sills around the edge of a door aperture). But don't scratch your head, and worry too much about spot-welding a joint if you really can't find a way to get at it—cut your losses, and use another method instead.

You can spot-weld steel to steel with almost any type of equipment, but only the professionals with very power-ful machinery can spot-weld aluminium to aluminium. We find that we need 50 KVA electrical capacity even to spot two sheets of 16SWG aluminium together, and really we need more than that.

On this old Jaguar E type, a new panel has just been spot-welded to a footwell. This is an ideal spot-welding location, with exposed flanges all facing outwards

It is rarely simple to apply spot-welds to a joint unless you have the appropriate arms. The arms used here have a long 'reach' so that they can be placed well behind the door shut face, which cannot be removed

There is no way that portable equipment, using domestic electrical power wiring, can spot-weld aluminium, so don't even attempt it. Nobody can spot-weld aluminium to steel either, it simply isn't possible.

If you are faced with relatively thin, 20SWG thickness sheet steel, you might just be able to spot-weld four thicknesses together, but a limit of three thicknesses would be more practical. You would find places where three thicknesses have to be spotted, say, where inner and outer sills also have a floor panel, or an internal reinforcement, at the same point.

Before even preparing to spot-weld panels together, make sure that the joints are clean, and that they mate together correctly. Cleanliness is all-important where welding is concerned, not because it is dangerous to use dirty or rusty panels, but because the welding is so much easier, and effective, if the surfaces are clean. You will soon know if the surfaces are not clean, for there will be a lot of spluttering and sparking, and the tips might even blow holes in the panel. The sparks, of course, could set light to anything inflammable on which they fall, so I hope you will always have a fire extinguisher *which you know how to operate* close by.

Although no pre-welding chemical coating is needed, you might like to consider using a zinc-based primer between the joints, where the paint will not be able to penetrate after welding. Because the primer is zinc-based, spot-welding will still take place through it, not too much will be burnt away, and you will retain some protection inside the joint which will help the body to last that much longer in the years to come.

Wear protective clothing, including clear-lensed goggles (or a clear mask), to guard against sparks, while you are doing the job. You don't need dark goggles (which are essential for arc-welding for instance), as efficient spot-welding produces virtually no sparking at all. If it does, something is wrong with the process, or the panels themselves.

Before starting to weld, clamp up the panels securely in the correct positions. This, I hope, is obvious advice,

New sills are being fitted in this restoration. To keep up appearances spot-weld them into place along their flanges, if at all possible

for once the very first secure spot-weld has been made, it is impossible to adjust the alignment of panels and flanges. Mole wrenches are perfectly adequate for this job, and naturally you shouldn't try to make do with just two or three. I like to use at least one 'floating' wrench, which I move along the panel joint as welding proceeds, close to the area to be tackled next.

For every particular job, you have to be sure that the tips (the actual points at which the welding takes place) are clean, in good condition and have the right shape. Generally, tips are copper and their ideal shape is something like a blunt-pointed pencil. Tips wear down, in use, and can be reshaped by using a special cutter, fixed into the chuck of an electric drill. These reproduce the correct shape, with a flat at the end which corresponds to the required spot size. Tips should be cleaned up regularly, for as they wear down the spotting area tends to enlarge. This tends to diffuse the power provided and weakens the spot-weld produced.

When sills are being welded into place, it is often possible to use spot-welding because the flanges are exposed at top and bottom

Above left **This small cluster of spot-welds fixed a rear panel to a boot surround. There are two staggered rows, presumably duplicating the layout found on the original, corroded bodyshell**

Left **When spot-welding new panels together, try to keep the spacings like those of the original car (if the evidence, and the old panels still survived when you started the job)**

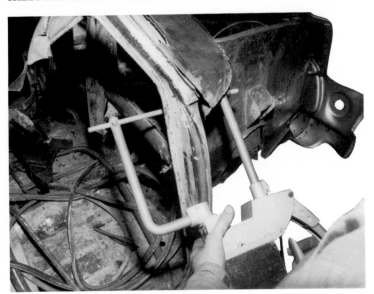

Above right **To get around this door pillar, two entirely different shapes of spot-welding arms were used—one long reach, one short**

Below right **You should always make sure that spot-welder electrodes just touch each other, with contact faces parallel, before you begin to tackle the job. Adjustment is easy**

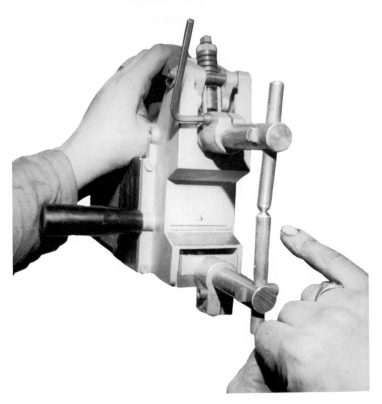

This is how the tip of both electrodes should look. There is a special shaping/cleaning tool mounted in the drill to make a quick and efficient job

With practice, you can get spot-welding results like the neat line on the left. A beginner might produce blotchy results, possibly by having the machine settings all wrong

Now you should be ready to set up the equipment, and to start spot-welding. Almost every machine has a table on the casing, which recommends power settings for any particular job—these vary with the thickness of material used, and the number of thicknesses to be spotted together.

What distance should there be between adjacent spots on the panel? There is no blanket advice for this, except to say that you should try to reproduce what the manufacturer used when the car was new. In general, spots are at least an inch apart, and probably more. Clearly there is no merit in using fewer spots than you found on the original panels, but is also fatally easy to try to cram too many into a particular area. I have found that if you try to spot very close to another spot, it is possible for the spotting

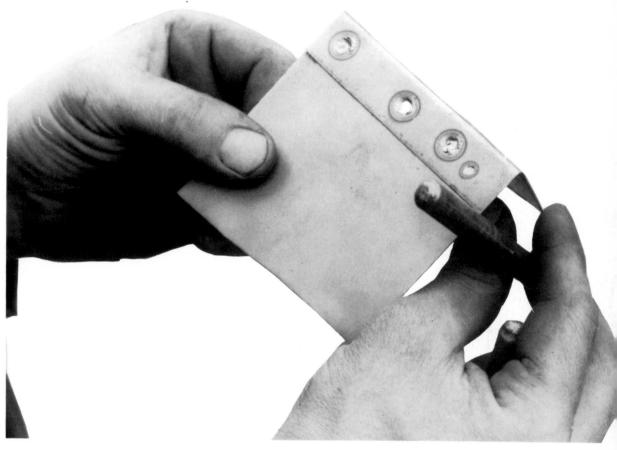

electrical current to divert itself through that other spot, and you might not get a satisfactory joint at all.

Spot-welding is done by the equipment firing a hefty eletrical charge through the metal, from tip to tip. The charge heats up the steel, which momentarily melts and welds one panel to the other. If the operator positions the tips properly, if the joint is clean and mating correctly, and the trigger is pulled, the spot-welding process is then automatic. The machine has its own built-in timer and does the spot-welding job according to the settings. As the electrical circuit is completed when the tips clamp the steel panels together, no extra wiring, or earthing connections, are needed.

If the welding current holds on for too long, it could easily punch a hole in the metal, as shown here, and it might also cause metal to be deposited on the electrodes too

Big machines for professional use tend to be water-cooled, which keeps the temperature of the equipment in check, but hand-operated welders have no real cooling. Naturally, the spot-welding process produces a great deal of heat, and without cooling this means that the tips might tend to distort.

Keep an eye on the tips, and if they start to get too hot, stop welding, take a break, or even tackle another short job while the equipment is cooling down again. Even though some of our works machines can weld for hours, we tend to do a job like this in stages.

At this stage I should mention that more modern cars are becoming rather complex, with some sections designed to crumple progressively in accidents, and others to be, and remain, very rigid indeed. This is achieved not only by the use of different thickness panels, and reinforcements, but by the number, and spacing, of spot-welds at joints. It is important, therefore, that you do not skimp (*or* try to be too clever) when spot-welding, as most patterns were designed with a purpose in mind.

It is inevitable, even with the best technique in the world, and on fresh, perfectly shaped panels, that spot-welding will lead to discoloration of the panel, and to a very slight depression in the panel at every spot. There is no trick way to make sure that this does not happen, although the use of a larger spot tip would minimize the problem.

One way to deal with these depressions on an outside panel would be to go in for some detailed planishing, using the pick hammer, but this can be a very lengthy or finicky process. The easiest way is to use some P38 body filler (I discuss the use of filler in a later chapter), or even to use some lead-loading.

Spot-welding, however, is one of the easiest metal crafts to learn, and if you use well-maintained equipment, correctly set, it should be possible to get acceptable spot-welds without a lot of trouble. As I have already said in earlier chapters, however, a bit of practice is never wasted. Experience, clean mating surfaces, and the correct application to the right place, will produce good spot-welds every time.

Chapter 7 | Welding, brazing and soldering

When constructing the bodyshell of a car, the alternative to fixing sheet metal panels together by spot-welding is to fuse them together, using intense heat. There are several ways of producing such localized heat, which fall into two major categories. One way is to produce a very hot flame by burning a mixture of gases—naturally enough, this is called gas-welding—and the other is to use the heat generated in a short arc of high-voltage electricity. Both have applications to the restoration of bodywork, and there is a choice of equipment available to the enthusiast amateur. Some types, however, are much too costly and sophisticated to even consider.

Gas-welding
Very briefly, in most cases gas-welding is tackled using oxy-acetylene equipment (or equipment which uses an alternative burning gas to acetylene), while arc-welding will either be done with the aid of a hand-held electrode holder and filler rod or (if you have a lot more money, and the need for more advanced equipment) with what is called CO_2-welding, where carbon dioxide gas is blown out around the filler rod as it is welding, to stop the new weld oxidizing at once.

(Well-equipped professional body shops often use argon arc-welding equipment too, but this is really very costly, and is not really within the scope of the home mechanic.)

In many cases, the home restorer will be able to tackle many jobs with a good gas-welding kit. Some years ago, in the UK, these could only be operated with the aid of large, high-pressure cylinders and appropriate fittings, hired out by the British Oxygen Co. Nowadays, though,

When welding in a part-section of a patch-piece, I would always recommend butt-welding— rather than forming a joggle, and having to lead-load or fill the resulting joint. This is a butt-welded joint in the sweep of a large panel

It is always advisable to tack two
panels together, before
attempting to form a long
continuous joint. In this case,
tacking is by brazing, which I
would not normally recommend,
but the *principle* of tacking is
well-illustrated

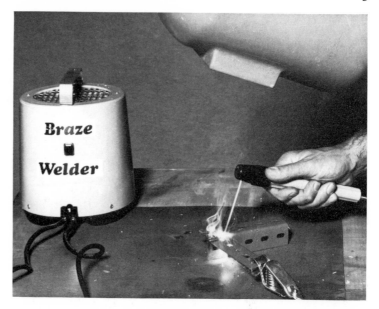

Above right **When striking an arc, you should always wear a full face mask like this—or you could damage your eyes. A mask also gives protection against flying sparks. The equipment shown here is very basic and not suitable for big projects.**

Left **This is a typical 'home'-restorer's' gas-welding kit, suitable for most car welding jobs. As you can see, it not only comes complete with a little stand for the bottles (which should always be stored upright) but a variety of nozzles, tools and explanatory leaflets**

not only do BOC produce a 'half-sized' Portapack kit (it used to be that unless you were in the 'trade' you couldn't buy—now you can), but there is a whole variety of portable 'private enterprise' kits whose UK prices vary from well under £100, to well over £200 at 1984 prices. Naturally, the gas bottles need to be renewed regularly, and on the sort of kits just mentioned they usually run out of gas in ten welding hours or so, though the oxygen itself lasts longer.

The hot flame is produced by feeding a mixture of gases though a nozzle and lighting up the mixture. One gas used is always oxygen, which does not burn itself, but which provides the means for the other gas to do so. (Oxygen, of course, is already present in air, but only makes up one-fifth of air, by content, and is not therefore concentrated enough to support an intense flame. The other four-fifths of air is nitrogen, which is virtually an inert gas as far as the business of burning is concerned.)

In most cases, the burning gas is acetylene, though there are alternatives, which tend to be more costly to produce (and, therefore, buy), and which are not found as often.

Most kits are supplied with carrying cradles, or trolleys,

This man is butt-welding two pieces of aluminium together, using a gas flame. For such a job goggles are needed, not a full face mask. In this case, too, note that there is no sparking of flaring from the weld point

and come complete with a choice of one or more nozzles, pipes linking the gas bottles to the nozzles, and pressure regulating valves. In some cases, too, you also get a spark lighter and a pair of goggles.

To carry out oxy-acetylene/gas-welding, you need to wear goggles at all times, not only to protect your eyes from the glare of the flame, but to protect them from any spitting and flaring which might occur if you are welding impure or 'dirty' panels. I hope I don't have to remind anyone that they should always wear the right sort of protective clothing; this should always include denim/heavy cotton overalls (never synthetics, which melt when heated up, with very nasty results), sturdy shoes or boots (not sneakers/trainers or wellies, please!), a cap over long hair, and a leather glove on the hand not wielding the torch itself.

No matter what sort of a hurry you are in, always check out the safety and integrity of the gear before beginning to use it, including the condition of the supply hoses, and the tightness of all the hose and nozzle connections. There is a right, and a wrong, way to light up the flame. You should always turn on the acetylene gas tap first, then use the spark lighter at the tip of the nozzle to fire it up in fresh air, when it will burn with a sooty flame. Turn up the pressure until you are just witnessing a trace of smoke, then gradually turn on the oxygen supply until the flame becomes more intense, with a hot tip at the nozzle itself and no smoke at all.

Basically there are three types of flame used—an oxidizing flame which has excess oxygen in the mixture, a neutral flame (half oxygen, half acetylene or equivalent), or a carburizing flame where there is an excess of acetylene. Normally the oxidizing flame is used when brazing (I discuss this later in the chapter), but in our business we do not use the carburizing type of flame at all. For the gas-welding of panels I would always use a neutral flame, where there is just a whitish rounded 'cone' flame at the tip of the nozzle.

Incidentally, at this stage I ought to emphasize that cleanliness of all the panels being welded is extremely important. If the metal being used is old, corroded or dirty, you might experience spluttering while welding is taking place, and any type of backfiring might tend to blow a hole through the weld.

Not only steel, but aluminium panels can be gas-welded together, but it is metallurgically impossible to weld steel to aluminium. Gas-welding aluminium panels is a more delicate business than it is with steel—you need a much 'softer' flame, for instance—because aluminium melts at a much lower temperature than does steel, and it is much more likely that you might blow a hole in the panel when welding along the line.

The obvious difference between the two materials is that you also need to use a flux before welding aluminium panels together. Flux is bought as a powder, mixed up into a paste with water (preferably distilled), then painted on to the edges of the panels before you start welding. Without the use of the flux, you just can't do the job at all. In all cases, the two panels should be securely clamped together, and to a workbench if possible, so that you have both arms

Using a BOC portable gas-welder on the sills of a Hillman Imp. This kit is typical of such equipment, with a trolley for supporting and transporting the bottles, and a stout case to hold the alternative nozzles and tools. Actually, I would have liked to see a fire extinguisher close to the job as well

free for the precision welding job.

In either case, if you have the misfortune to blow a hole into the weld (they tend to be much larger holes in aluminium, but in steel they will usually only be pin-sized holes), these can be filled in, with patience and suitable filler rods.

As I have said before in this book, do not even consider tackling the actual welding jobs themselves until you have gained the necessary experience, and have practiced on scrap panels. This little book certainly cannot teach you how to weld, but it can certainly provide you with basic advice on methods. The object, with gas-welding, is always to neatly fuse panels together along the joint line, achieving good penetration and leaving as little extra weld as possible, so as to obviate lengthy smoothing and planishing when the job is done. Of course it always helps to have your torch tips in good condition (they should last a lifetime if properly maintained), and always to store the kit safely when it is not in use. The bottles, for instance, should always be stored vertically—this being ensured if they are kept in their cradles or trolleys.

If you intend to gas-weld a lengthy joint, do not make the mistake of starting at one end and working steadily towards the other, for with thin metal panels being used this will almost automatically mean that there will be heat distortion, and the fit and finish will not be acceptable. It is always best to start the process by tack-welding—by welding the joint in short lengths, several inches apart. This is really done for the same reason that two pieces of cloth are pinned together before they are machine sewn—it makes sure that nothing moves out of place while the welding (sewing!) is going on.

When butt-welding a patch piece, or a part panel, to the original, I would tack the metal every inch or so, tidy it up, then virtually weld the rest together without even using a filler rod, or just use it very sparingly. There should then only be a small amount of weld to clean off before you start planishing the area. That, by the way, is the classic way used by craftsmen building up hand-beaten bodies to this day—we often uncover the evidence when stripping out a modern Ferrari for restoration. The same advice applies for any such gas-welding job; you cannot afford to get the

welding process wrong, for once done the joint is permanent, and you would have to resort to the hammer and cold
chisel, or grinding wheel, approach to separate what you
have just welded.

There are technical college evening classes which will
give you a good grounding in gas-welding expertise, and
you will also find written advice in many libraries, but in
the end, your success as a welder will depend on the
amount of practice you get at the job.

For gas-welding of exterior sheet metal panels (not great
thick sheets, as found in chassis frames and in the 'chassis
legs' or structural undersides of a monocoque)—after you
have tacked the joint together, and made sure that the joint
is still correctly made, then you can start working along
to fill up the gaps.

Assuming you are right-handed, hold the torch in that
hand, and the filler rod in your left, and bring them
together, almost like a knife and fork, at the point where
you intend to start welding. When tacking, you will already
have discovered that it is only the brilliant little 'tip' which
is the 'working' part of the flame, so it follows that the torch
tip will almost have to be touching the joint.

With the torch tip angled towards the left, and the filler
rod strategically placed just ahead of it, heat up one spot
until a small 'pool' of molten metal appears (when this
cools down it will form the weld holding the two panels
together). Then begin to 'push' the pool and the red hot
areas of panel to each side of it, slowly but surely towards
the left, retracting the filler rod in front of it, dabbing in
as necessary to produce the correct condition. Knowing
when to add filler rod and how fast to keep moving the
torch are things you can only really learn with experience.
You can only go as quickly as the metal will let you and
after a time this will become second nature to you.

You should need to make only one pass of the joint, you
should concentrate on the local area at all times, be sure
that you are laying down enough, and are getting penetration. If you can still see the panel joint where the two
pieces of metal have come together, then you haven't got
the penetration correct. You should certainly never need
to weld along both sides.

Two obvious words of warning—while you are welding, always have an efficient fire extinguisher on hand, and be sure not to try to handle newly-welded metal only seconds after you have completed the job. It is very easy indeed for a novice to burn himself when gas-welding, especially if he is not careful where he points the torch while it is switched on. Beware—both body sealants and trim are very flammable.

Arc-welding

Straight away I should say that professional body shops rarely use simple arc-welding techniques for body sheet work. Generally speaking arc-welding is now limited to use on heavier gauge material. We would tend to use CO_2 equipment, which is very versatile indeed, as it can cope with anything from thin sheets to $\frac{1}{4}$ in. (6 mm) thick plate, but the snag is that there tends to be quite a bit of weld build up which has to be cleaned down, and tidied up, before you can continue to work the metal.

In the case of simple arc-welding, or Argon/CO_2-welding, the local heat is achieved by persuading an electrical arc to jump a very short distance between the equipment's filler rod and the panel joint itself. This is done because the metal panel has already been connected to the welding equipment by an earthing clamp.

Arc-welding is done with an electrode holder to which filler rod is fixed, while CO_2-welding involves a type of

For minor welding jobs, the light-duty 'Welder's Mate' arc-welding kit could be powered from two 12-volt batteries. The clamp on the right of the drawing provides an earth return to complete the necessary electrical circuit

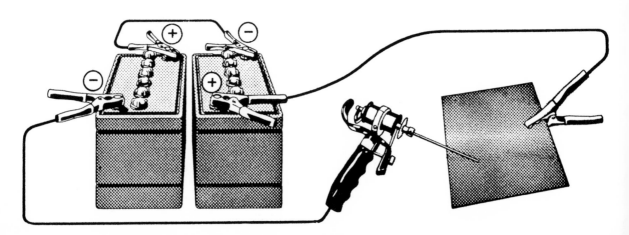

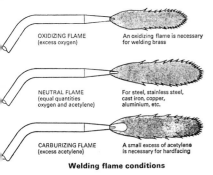

OXIDIZING FLAME
(excess oxygen)

An oxidizing flame is necessary
for welding brass

NEUTRAL FLAME
(equal quantities
oxygen and acetylene)

For steel, stainless steel,
cast iron, copper,
aluminium, etc.

CARBURIZING FLAME
(excess acetylene)

A small excess of acetylene
is necessary for hardfacing

Welding flame conditions

**This illustrates the three
different types of flame available
from a gas-welding nozzle. For
almost every metalworking job
use a neutral flame, with equal
proportions of oxygen and
acetylene (or its equivalent)**

'gun' out of which steel wire is fed from a reel on the machine which strikes the arc, while at the same time a shroud of inert carbon dioxide gas (CO_2), or a similar mixture of inert gases, is pumped out around this wire to shield it from the oxygen in the atmosphere. In the case of CO_2-welding equipment, industrial-type three-phase electrical power wiring may be needed, the equipment is much more bulky and complicated (for a high-pressure gas bottle, and an electrically driven reel of wire is involved), and the costs can be high.

The only practical option for the home-based restorer is simple arc-welding, for which several kits compatible with household electrical wiring are available. Naturally, you get what you pay for, but the better ones not only include a face mask, electrode holder, earth clamp and clips, wire brushes, a selection of electrodes *and* a detailed instruction guide, but they can be adapted to several uses.

The electrical circuitry of an arc-welder is very simple. The machine is plugged into the power circuits, perhaps through a heavy-duty transformer, the earthing wire and clamp is fixed to the panel to be welded, and the 'business' end which you will hold makes the circuit when it is brought very close, but *not* quite touching, the metal. The welding 'torch' is really little more than a pistol grip pair of pliers, with the rod clamped to it. There is a wide choice of flux-covered welding rods—that for normal sheet metal work is 0·8 mm in diameter, but for much thicker material to be welded you can get up to $\frac{1}{16}$ in. or $\frac{1}{8}$ in. diameter rods.

When the arc strikes, it is very bright indeed, and for that reason you must use a very strongly tinted visor or goggles. The emissions are so intense that it is also even advisable to cover your arms up to protect them from the light, and make sure that no reflected light can get in around the side of the lenses. Since arc-welding is only a one-handed job if the panels are clamped down in advance, you have one hand free, and personally I prefer to use a big hand-held mask rather than wear goggles.

It is a dangerous false economy to try to make do with the goggles you find adequate for gas-welding. With gas-welding goggles, it is often possible to see across the workshop, but when wearing an arc-welding mask, you cannot

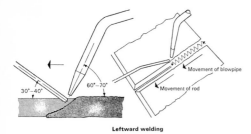

Leftward welding

When gas-welding, if you are using your right hand to hold the torch, the best method is to 'push' the flame and the puddle of molten metal to the left, if possible, with the filler rod just ahead of the flame. Practice will make perfect!

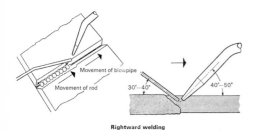

Rightward welding

When welding thick sections together (it doesn't often apply to bodyshell restoration, as much as chassis) the torch can often slowly be drawn to the right, with the filler rod following it up. This sometimes gives a better spread of heat over a thick joint

see out of it all before the arc is struck. The awkward question I often have to answer—if the mask is so opaque, how do you see where to strike the arc or point the rod?

This is why a hand-held mask is so useful, or one where the lens pivots up on to your forehead. You get as close up to the point as possible before striking the arc (only experience will tell you how close that is) draw the mask across your eyes, then strike the arc, and suddenly you *will* be able to see what you are doing again!

There should always be a small gap between the joint and the filler rod—rather like in a sparking plug—for if they touch the filler rod will tend to stick, and when the weld cools down you will be in a great deal of trouble! Incidentally, as I have already mentioned regarding spot-welding equipment, on arc-welding equipment there will be various settings and adjustments which can be made, to take account of the metal thicknesses to be welded together; if you follow these recommendations carefully, then you stand the best possible chance of producing workman-like results.

As with gas-welding, so with arc-welding techniques—I would recommend that you start by tacking the two panels together with small blobs of weld, a few inches apart, so as to minimize distortion, before beginning to draw lines of weld along the joint from tack to tack. This is not a very speedy process—to do the job properly, with care, at the recommended settings, it might take you up to 15 minutes or so to do a foot of weld at a time.

Don't allow yourself to get bored, and do try to give the equipment a rest, to cool down, from time to time. By the way, I don't recommend that you try to cool the weld down quickly with cold water, as that will only encourage a start to the inevitable rusting process. There is no doubt that actually striking the arc (one good way is to swing the electrode in a gentle curve until it just grazes the surface, and lift it off very slightly as it sparks for the first time), and being able to keep the electrode *just* out of touching range are two of the most difficult features—if you are physically tired from too much concentrated welding, you may not do the job right. If the electrode ever sticks to the workpiece, an electrical short circuit is caused. This *must* be broken quickly, either by rapidly twisting the rod from side to side to break it, or by disconnecting the earth.

Technique only comes with practice—it is easy to forget, at first, that the welding rod in the hand-held electrode is consumed rapidly, so that the electrode has to be lowered gradually, as it passes along the weld joint, for instance. If you travel along the joint too fast the welded 'bead' will be too small, if you are too slow it will be too bulky, if the current is too low there will not be enough penetration, and if too high you may tend to burn craters or even holes in the metal. There are no easy solutions—practice, and then more practice will help in the long run.

By the way, it is not possible to arc-weld aluminium to aluminium.

If it is at all possible, you should always clamp two pieces of metal together before beginning to tack them into place. In this case, not only a vice, but clamps have been brought into play

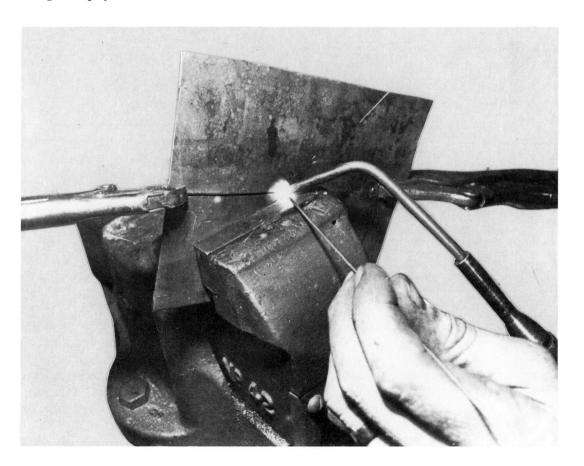

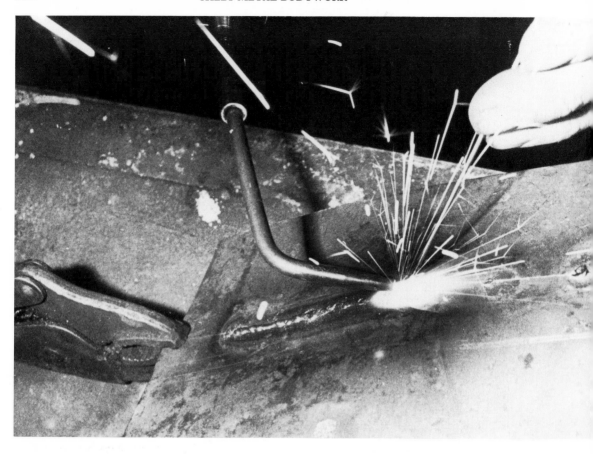

Perhaps a bit more sparking than I would like to see, but this shot demonstrates how the gas-welding torch and the filler rod are both held closely together, near the line of the weld itself

Brazing

Whereas welding involves fusing two pieces of metal together, brazing merely 'glues' them together. Using a gas-welding torch, a brass rod can be melted and used to stick two pieces together. Use the torch to heat the joint red, but not melt either piece, then touch the fluxed brazing rod to that point, whereupon it will melt into the joint. It is therefore an easier process than gas-welding, but in our workshop we would not contemplate using it. A DIY application, perhaps, would be to use brass to infiltrate two joints which have been joggled together. This only ever applies to steel, because you cannot braze aluminium to aluminium, as they are incompatible.

Brazing really has no place in the assembly of a car, par-

ticularly where the joints are stressed, for the bond is not nearly as strong as it would be if welded.

Soldering

As with the use of brass, soldering is a very low-technology 'second division' method of fixing panels together in the body of a motor car, and I would not normally recommend the technique. You could, I suppose, solder into a joggle after it had been spot-welded, but it does not add strength, but merely covers up the work already done.

In a car, soldering is usually found in cooling radiators and in the jointing of some petrol tanks, but this is mostly for sealing purposes, after a welding process has already been carried out.

On a MIG-welder there is a reel of wire which feeds directly to the pipe of the torch, which is being held close to the pressure adjuster. To get the MIG-welder working, the hand grip is squeezed, when wire begins to be fed automatically forward into the flame

Chapter 8 | Finishing touches

All the heavy, back-breaking work is now over, and the bodyshell should once again be looking complete. But after all the cutting out, trimming back, the patching and welding in of new sections, or the addition of complete new panels, the body might still look untidy. In fact you might be discouraged—from an old and rusting mess, you will now have produced a new and partly shining mess.

There will be new metal next to old metal, new lines of welding alongside old lines, and quite a number of blemishes which you have not been able to eliminate. Even if you have become a very skilled panel beater by this time, quite a lot of the shell will still need detail improvement before it is ready to be painted.

Don't let this get you down, for it is now time to apply the finishing touches. You need to get rid of all the rough edges, the imperfect matching and the small uneven patches, that no amount of careful metalworking has been able to eliminate. Don't worry—it happens to all of us. Now is the time to use one of two local treatments—lead-loading, or body filler. Both can be used on steel bodywork, but generally speaking it is only possible to use filler on aluminium bodies.

Your object is to apply one or other of these materials to small areas of the body, to smoothe them out completely, so that you literally cannot trace where one panel meets the next, or where a patch of new metal has been welded to the old. After lead-loading or filling, you should be able to pass your fingers over a panel area and find it as smooth as it will be after the paint has been applied.

Modern mass-produced bodyshells use much less lead-loading than was the case some years ago. This is not

Above right **One of the many tidying-up jobs to be completed on a restored bodyshell is to get rid of excess weld from new joints, particularly if you have been gas- or MIG-welding. You can rarely get into a comfortable position while doing so! It appears as though the operator in this photograph has no eye protection. He has, in fact, an eye shield. Always wear protective clothing.**

Below right **Not much actual construction to do now on this GTO, but there will be a lot more filling to complete, particularly on the rear quarters, before the painting process can begin**

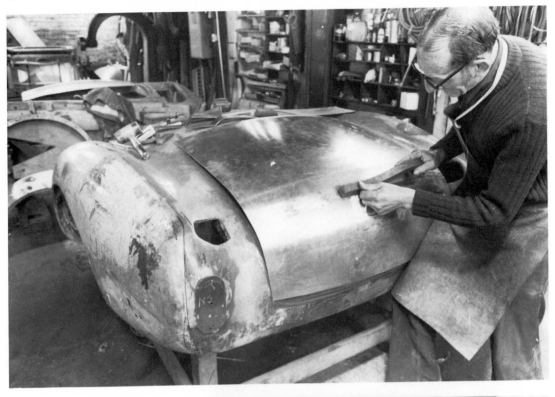

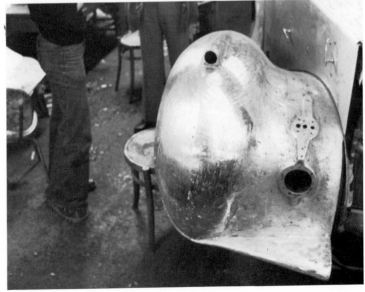

Above **Using a Dreadnought file
on the boot lid of an AC Cobra.
This process reveals the
remaining high and low spots,
and you should only start to use
filler when the panel beating is
completely finished**

Right **A very deeply shaped
separate front wing, with quite a
lot of lead-loading already done.
More work, probably using filler,
will be needed on the inner
valance**

Above **Evidence of lead-loading** *and* **filler on the top of this BMW front wing, which is now almost ready for painting**

Left **The rear end of this Porsche 356 is finished, with a new tail section having been fabricated, welded to the existing shell and expertly lead-loaded to hide all evidence of the joints**

Above **After lead-loading, it is impossible to know that the wheel arch joint to the door shut face of this car was ever completely corroded away, with holes breaking through**

Above right **A complete patch piece has been welded into this front wing, above and behind the centre line of the wheel arch, as well as another patch close to the door hinge face. Lead-loading has carefully smoothed over the joints**

because the process is unsatisfactory, but because panel matching has been improved progressively, and because there are some health risks involved in the grinding down of the lead itself. For body restoration, however, lead-loading's only alternative is the use of body filler. Lead is an ideal 'filler' for areas that you haven't been able to planish, for welded joints that are not quite as you would want them, and for smoothing out imperfections in the body. Obvious places where lead is invaluable are where roof panels meet windscreen or quarter pillars, or where boot lid surrounds meet tonneau panels.

The lead is bought in half-kilogram sticks, and is actually not pure lead, but a combination of lead and tin. Before you can start applying it to the body, however, it is necessary to 'tin' the areas involved, with a tinning material bought as a proprietary compound. Basically this is powered lead in a flux; to apply, brush it on to the surface

Above **Once the area to be lead-loaded is clean, paint all over it with a paste-like preparation, a 'tinning' material. When applied, this will help the lead to adhere properly**

Left **Once the tinning has been applied, you should start applying lead without delay. This operator is using a welding torch to make heat, which I would not recommend—the all-over heat of a simple blowlamp is much preferable**

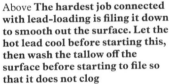

Above **The hardest job connected with lead-loading is filing it down to smooth out the surface. Let the hot lead cool before starting this, then wash the tallow off the surface before starting to file so that it does not clog**

Above right **The finished job will look like this, with no high spots or low spots to spoil the smooth change of contour. But it takes a great deal of delicate work to arrive at this condition, ready for painting to start**

as a paste, warm over the surface with a simple blowlamp (*not* a welding torch, the heat is too localized), let the paste melt, then wipe it over with a rag. This gives a small layer of lead on the metal, and ensures that the main application of lead from the stick will adhere satisfactorily.

You don't have to leave the result to cool down (you always need the metal to be warm, to a certain degree, while lead-loading), but you can now get straight on with the application of lead. Taking the stick of lead in one hand, and an ordinary blowlamp (we always use the propane-powered variety) in the other, begin to 'puddle' the metal, which melts quite readily, on to the area to be smoothed over.

The real skill of lead-loading, particularly if the panel involved is vertical not horizontal, is to get it all on to the job and not dripping on to the floor! Once you have a patch of lead in place, you have to start working it into shape. To do this use a wooden spatula of an appropriate shape (I actually have different shapes for different jobs). These need to be made from a hardwood, not a soft wood with open grains, and to ensure that the lead does not stick to them I smear them with tallow fat to provide a lubricant. All the time that you are using a spatula, the blowlamp should be in use to keep the lead in a soft, putty-like state (not fully liquid or flowing freely). It always helps if you can keep as large an area as possible 'on the move', as it were—this can only be achieved by using a blowlamp, for a welding torch flame would be much too concentrated.

Once enough lead is in place on the chosen area, filling up cracks, or covering over welded joints, it is time to smooth it out to the desired contour. I would always recommend that you wear a simple face mask when carrying out the lead-loading process, by the way, particularly when you start the filing and discing down, which makes lead particles fly into the air.

You can never take too much trouble, in getting the lead to the correct profile—and don't worry if you make a mistake and take off too much material, as it is easy merely to apply more fresh lead on top of the existing patch. Use a file if you can, then paper, and aim to finish the job so that there are no score marks in the surface.

The modern alternative to lead-loading is to use body filler. In the UK, this means using David's P38, which is sold in paste form, in tins of various sizes—any motor accessory shop should be able to supply. Because it is based on the fibreglass resin principle, a tube of hardener is also needed, and once the two compounds are mixed, the result tends to 'go off' quite rapidly.

It's a pity that the use of body filler, indiscriminately, is associated with bodging, for it is a very versatile material for the restorer. I agree that a lot of very nasty, very temporary body repairs are done using P38 and fibreglass sheets, but if it is used correctly, and delicately, it can be extremely useful indeed.

Before applying the filler, read product instructions carefully, mix hardener in the correct proportions, then apply it just to the area you are working on. After it has hardened, the work of smoothing it out has to be done, perhaps with a file to get close to the profile, then with papers, of progressively finer grades, so that no scoring marks are left.

As with lead-loading, if you are over-enthusiastic and take off too much filler, it is easily possible to add more fresh filler on top of it. Incidentally, whereas lead-loading material needs a 'tinned' surface to allow it to stick, body

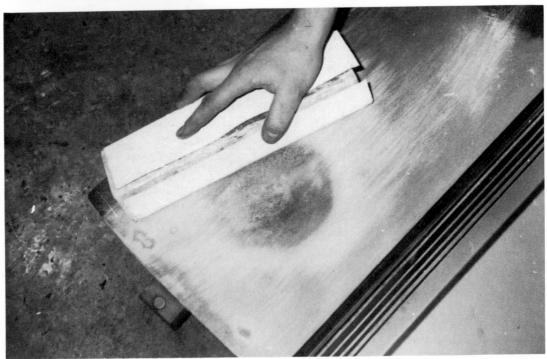

Above left **A blowlamp is being used here, on an already-leaded rear wing, to soften up a patch of material prior to it being smoothed out**

Below left **Once a depression has been identified, ready for filling, the whole adjoining surface needs to be smoothed down carefully— here a long wooden block surrounded with flattening paper was employed**

Above right **Filler being applied across the depression, rather more than is ideally needed, for you will have ample opportunity to flat it all down again**

Below right **Flattening down should always be done by hand— the skin is a remarkably sensitive indication of smoothness in a panel—using finer and finer papers on wooden blocks**

filler needs no more than clean, fresh metal.

Which process is best for which part of the car? Lead-loading requires heat, if rather general heat, so there is always a tendency for a panel to sink or distort a little when lead is being applied, and this normally means that you can not apply it in the centre of a panel. Filler can be used anywhere without such problems cropping up (and in any case, you have no option if you are preparing an aluminium body for painting).

I hope I don't need to emphasize that both materials, lead and body filler, should only be applied to bare metal, never on to old paint, or old filler. Perhaps you could get them to stick, but I would neither recommend it nor guarantee the life of the repair.

Never think that you are wasting time when working on the finishing touches, for it is attention to detail at this stage which will help to ensure an even, glossy and long-lasting paint finish to the restored car—as good or even better than it ever had when it left the factory in the first place. Near enough, at this point, is not good enough, for blemishes and imperfect shapes will always show through the paint, no matter how many coats are applied. In the companion book in this series, Miles Wilkins has spelt out the many ways in which paintwork quality might be compromised.

So now the job is done and, hopefully, the bodyshell of your car will be clean, smooth, pristine and ready for painting and reassembly to take place. Was it all worthwhile? Was it really worth spending those hundreds of hours on preparation, planishing, and corrosion-proofing? Believe me, it was—but if you decided to take short-cuts, you will soon discover the pitfalls, when corrosion starts to break out over again. Then you will have to go back to page 1!

Index